FIRMLY PLANTED PUBLICATIONS

An imprint of Equipped for Life Ministries, Dallas, Texas

I0081090

The Offer of a Second Inheritance

and a new life to obtain it

B. Dale Taliaferro

The Offer of a Second Inheritance
Published by Firmly Planted Publications
An imprint of Equipped for Life Ministries

Copyright © 2017 by B. Dale Taliaferro
International Standard Book Number:
978-1-950072-13-2

Cover Art by Hannah Gleghorn Design, Frisco, Texas

Printed copies sold at Logos Book Store, 6620 Snider Plaza, Dallas, Texas, 75205-3483

For information:
Equipped for Life Ministries
P.O. Box 12013
Dallas, Texas 75225
U.S.A.

Library of Congress Number:

Revised Edition 2019

Acknowledgements

I am so thankful for all the individuals who have made comments to me either in a personal edit of this manuscript or as we discussed the material together. Your insights and editorial comments have made this a better book. I especially want to thank Carol Trebes and Bret Burdette for their meticulous editorial comments on the manuscript. Even though I had read and re-read the manuscript at least six to eight times, my eyes and mind got so accustomed to what was being said that I could not see the grammatical or spelling mistakes that were still present. And, of course, where would I be without my good friend Maritza Ortiz who formatted the manuscript for publication? Your help was such a blessing because you did what I could not begin to undertake on my own. And you did it at a time when your own life was overflowing with new commitments. So, thank you all. I am truly blessed to have you beside me.

Table of Contents

Preface to the Revised Edition   1

Introduction   3

Section One – Proofs that Jesus Was the Messiah   9

Chapter 1: Declared by Many to be the Messiah,
      the Son of God   11

Chapter 2: Fulfilled Prophecies Require It   21

    A Man   24
    From the Lineage of Abraham   26
    From the Tribe of Judah   27
    From the Family of David   28
    Born in Bethlehem of Judea   31
    The Time of Messiah's Coming and Rejection   32
    The Conclusion Seems Apparent   34

Chapter 3: Jesus' Ministry Fulfills the Messianic
      Expectations   37

Chapter 4: Jesus' Death and Resurrection Prove
      His Messiahship   45

Section Two – Jesus Describes God and His Will   49

Chapter 5: Jesus Came to Explain God's Character   51

Chapter 6: Jesus Came to Explain God's Universal Will   61

Section Three – Jesus Came to Redeem   77

Chapter 7: Jesus Came to Free Mankind   79

Chapter 8: Jesus, a Scapegoat? Or Not!   87

Section Four – Jesus Came to Give Life   95

Chapter 9: His Life is Related to His Kingship   97

Chapter 10: Eternal Life, a Taste of Kingdom Life!   105

Chapter 11: His Life is Supernaturally Powerful   113

Chapter 12: His Life is Transformative   119

Chapter 13: His Life is Sufficient for all Trials   125

**Section Five – A New World View Demands
a New Witness**   129

Chapter 14: God's Original Purpose for All Men   131

    Created in His Image for Fellowship and Service   134
    God, Partial in His Judgments?   135

Chapter 15: Sin Did Not Change God's Purpose for Man   143

Chapter 16: Man May Stray from God   149

Chapter 17: God's Message for an Ever-Shrinking World   155

Preface to the Revised Edition

This series of books was written during my spiritual journey. As a result, I now find the need to go back through each volume and make some necessary corrections and updates. I really didn't understand how many preconceived ideas that I was working from and that were still hindering my comprehension of the real message of the Bible. I still needed to confront several issues and hold them under the microscope of God's Word. For the sake of simplicity, I will summarize those issues here:

1. I developed a better understanding of the historical situations of some very important passages which changed my thinking relative to their meaning. As a result, the unpardonable sin has been revised. Basically, the unpardonable sin is a rejection of Jesus as the Messiah by the first century Jewish people, resulting in a delay of their earthly kingdom, promised to them by God in the OT, and to their missing entering into that kingdom in their mortal bodies.

2. I finally was able to move past my theological prejudices concerning Acts 16:31 and Eph. 2:8-9 by understanding salvation and faith Biblically. As a result, I have found that the Bible does not describe a person as being saved from hell because salvation never refers to a deliverance from hell once-for-all or in any other way. Consequently, these two classic passages on salvation have nothing to do with a rescue from hell with a promise of heaven. Those ideas have been read into these passages without any substantiation.

1

3. Since no one was ever described as a "saved person" by *initially* trusting in Jesus, I am led to reframe from doing that as well. I eventually realized that even the apostles were not described as "saved persons" after they had initially trusted in Jesus. *Salvation is not a standing or status before God that guarantees a person a heavenly home and an escape from hell.* Nor is it a permanent, unchangeable condition that is reached by initially (or continually) trusting in Jesus. We can be saved from temptations and sins, but we can't be saved from hell and given heaven due to a simple trust in Jesus.

4. Finally, I realized that while there is no concept in the NT that can be likened to the traditional idea of a "saved person" in Christian teachings, there is a NT concept of a *salvation that is taking place presently.* As a result, it is biblical to describe people as being saved from temptations and sins but not as having been saved once for all from hell with a guarantee of heaven. Since the Bible doesn't do that, neither should we. It is easy to see how this reinforces the new understanding of Acts 16:30-31 and Eph. 2:8-9.

With these discoveries, I was able to reach a consistent concept of salvation with nothing but the Bible as my guide. **The biggest correction that I have needed in these volumes is to distinguish between a *spiritual* salvation that is defined as an ongoing deliverance from temptations and sins from the traditional, but mistaken, idea of a *spiritual* salvation that supposedly takes place at the moment of initial faith in Jesus and that supposedly obtains a deliverance from hell.** While the former is clearly Biblical; the latter is a creation by men alone.

Introduction

This book is, in a way, a summary of much of what has been written in the first four volumes. But it is also an attempt to set forth four major reasons for Jesus' coming in His first Advent. It is understood that in one sense everything that Jesus did and said could be listed as a reason for His first appearing. The reason for saying that is everything that He said was given to Him by the Father to say, and everything that He did was part of the will of God for Him to accomplish. I have simplified the study by breaking down the intentionality of His coming into four categories or reasons.

The first reason for His coming was to convince everyone that He was indeed the promised Messiah. This reason alone, if it is given its proper consideration, should cause us to rethink much of what we believe. He came as the Jewish Messiah. Consequently, whatever He did must be related to His Messiahship. If He is detached from that office, His person and ministry cannot be properly understood. So, for example, He came to *save* only in the sense that the Jewish Messiah would *save*. To construct a *salvation* different from the one revealed in the OT is to misunderstand what He came to do and to attribute to Him goals that He never came to accomplish. That is, I believe, exactly what orthodox Christianity has done.

The second reason for His coming was to explain the character and will of God the Father. Over time many differing pictures of God have been formed by different people groups around the world. Jesus came to explain the Father so we could understand Him better and depend upon Him more fruitfully. When Jesus clarified through the writings of His disciples the *Father's universal will for all men*, He confirmed a standard that was already in place and had been used for all men in the world. This universal will of God has been clearly revealed by God so that all men are without excuse. God is drawing all men to Himself by His continuing communication to each person, inviting him into His presence for personal blessings as they serve Him.

The third reason that Jesus came the first time was to redeem man. The two short chapters that cover this issue summarize many of the ideas developed in volume four of this series, *Freedom through the Cross*. Jesus died to free man from the consequences of his first sin, providing a way back into God's presence and a forgiveness for all that he had done.

The wonderfully astounding results of the death of Jesus Christ on the cross completely freed man to walk with God his whole life, from birth to death. Such a walk will be greatly rewarded now in this life and in the age to come, the millennial reign of Jesus, the Jewish Messiah-King. The idea of redemption follows the Bible's first use of it for the exodus of the nation of Israel from its slavery in Egypt. Hence, redemption, like all the other soteriological terms, has to do with this life, and not with some possible consequence that might come upon a person after death.

The fourth reason that Jesus came is the key to everything. *He came to give His life **to** us, not just **for** us.* This life is the most profound gift that Jesus offered to those who believe in Him as the Jewish Messiah. It is under-appreciated today because it is hardly experienced by those who possess it, and rarely taught by those responsible for its communication. When it is experienced, that experience is nothing short of Jesus living His life through the one who is trusting in Him. The apostle Paul described it just this way early in his ministry as he wrote to those who had trusted in Jesus in Galatia: "...it is no longer I who live but Christ lives in me" (Gal. 2:20).

Jesus came to give the person who believes in Jesus the resources to get through this life in an extraordinary fashion, spiritually speaking. *This life* grants a power for living that is beyond the imagination of most personal counselors, Christian and secular. What Jesus is offering can't be obtained through any other means that man may suggest. *This life* is nothing short of phenomenal.

How would you like to experience love, joy, peace, patience, kindness, goodness, gentleness, faithfulness, and self-control in *every single situation* in your life?

How would you like to forgive those who, so far, have been unforgiveable?

How would you like to have the ability to endure, and not be hurt or traumatized by, a wrong done to you, regardless of how severe it might be?

How would you like to be able to rejoice and be glad when others ridicule and persecute you, saying all kinds of evil things about you falsely?

How would you like to encounter the most dreadfully stressful situations without becoming anxious or fearful?

How would you like to be able to love even your enemies?

All this and so much more is available to the one who is willing to learn how to trust in Jesus to live His life through him.

But most of all, how would you like to experience right now, today, the life that will be lived in *the age to come*, in that future age when Messiah is physically present, ruling over all the world?

How would you like to feel the love of God in tangible ways?

How would you like to have a sense of His presence and know that the invisible God is standing before you and your difficulties?

How would you like to know for sure that the one, true God is your God and that you are His child experientially? This is what Jesus came to give those who believe in Him. Is this your experience?

All that Jesus did and all that He taught provide each person with a way back into God's presence in order to experience the Father's great love for him during his earthly life. Experiencing that love makes us whole, gives us a new purpose in life, and brings meaning to every situation that we have to face.

This life of fellowship and obedience is actually a *stewardship* that has been entrusted to each person coming into the world. The same is true of the life that is given to the one who believes in Jesus. All stewards must be evaluated for faithfully performing the stewardship delegated to them. If you have done well, your performance (and you yourself) will be justified for the last time as God evaluates your entire life. If you have done poorly, there will be consequences received at the Judgment Seat of Christ to help conform you into the image of Jesus Christ. But they may not all be pleasant as the rich man discovered after he and Lazarus had died.

But let's be clear on this one fact: this new understanding of the message of the Bible is not about working one's way to heaven. In fact, the message of the Bible isn't about heaven (or hell) at all. No one needs to think about heaven, be concerned about getting to heaven, or fearfully paranoid about what will happen after he dies. The afterlife will take care of itself. This present, earthly life is about walking with a loving heavenly Father as you obey His will. If a person does those two things, he should not be overwhelmed by this life nor fearful about the afterlife. And to ensure that each person who believes in Jesus can do that, a new life is given through God's Spirit moment by moment. Experiencing this life is an extraordinary adventure!

When the prodigal son returned home, he was given an opportunity to earn *a second inheritance*. He had thrown away his first one through prodigal living. But now his father welcomed him home and provided everything he needed to gain another inheritance. In the father's own words, my prodigal son, who was always my son whether he lived in my house or in a distant land, was *dead*, having *separated* himself from me, but is now *alive*, having *come back* to me. This renewed relationship would provide the basis for obtaining another inheritance through the hard work of obedience, given in a loving relationship.

The salient point of all this is the simple truth that regardless of how poorly a person may have lived his life, if he returns to God and begins to walk by faith with Him again, he can not only move past his former struggles, but he can experience a life that he has never known before. If he lives by *this life*, his perspective on his circumstances, his search for meaning and purpose, and his ability to handle emotionally, spiritually, and physically the trial before him changes. In short, living by *this life* is rewarded by God in this world with blessings and in the age to come, when the Messiah returns to set up His kingdom, with wonderful opportunities for service.

These opportunities for service constitute the wonderful *second inheritance*. A wasted life can be rebuilt by the power of the life that God will give a person who believes in Jesus moment by moment. If you have believed that He is God's promised Messiah for Israel, you possess the life that can deliver you spiritually from every trial or difficulty that you face in life. Not only can you get through the trial, you can get through it with confidence, peace, and a joy that is inexpressibly full. God not only forgives; He also provides for a wonderfully abundant life that is able to accrue *a second inheritance*.

Section One

Proofs that Jesus Was the Messiah

Chapter 1

Declared by Many to be the Messiah, the Son of God

The allusions to the Christian perspective on the world were too many not to notice in the movie *Matrix*. Throughout the movie a world of sensory perception was contrasted to an underlying world of reality. What you saw, tasted, and felt was fake; what you couldn't see, taste, or feel was real. The world of sensory perception was misleading, keeping from you the truth of the real world; but this sensory world was so tantalizing, meeting the natural, self-centered desires that spring up from within the soul of man, that mankind entrapped itself in a world of delusion, manipulated and controlled by outside agents.

A deliverer was to arise to save all people from those who had imposed the fake world upon everyone to deceive them into thinking that there was nothing else that was real but what they could see, taste, and feel. When that deliverer appeared, he would be identified by several prophecies made about him. He would have super-powers, and one of his peers would fall in love with him. When these things became self-evidently true, all those of the rebellion knew for certain that "the one" had come to effect their deliverance.

In a similar but much more profound way, the promised Messiah of God would be identified. There were over three hundred prophecies made about Him to help those living at the time of His appearance to recognize Him. Of these prophecies, we will look at only a very few in the next chapter. But these will be enough to narrow the field of potential candidates down to just one, lone Candidate. Even though many others would appear on the scene at the same time in the first century, none could fulfill the prophetic prescriptions uniquely designed to infallibly describe the Christ of God.

Identifying the Messiah, promised to Israel by God, as the Anointed one (or the Christ) may seem for many Christians to be a strange way to begin our study. Many naturally connect *Christ* with *Christian*. But when they are reminded that the Greek term Christ is a synonym for the Hebrew term Messiah, many become a bit puzzled. Why does it matter that Jesus was the *Jewish Messiah*? Isn't it enough to believe that He was sent by God as the anointed one, as the Christ, to be our *Savior*? That is a profound question and should be carefully considered Biblically.

As long as we understand that Jesus' work of saving is related to His Messiahship, believing in Him as Savior is fine. But it is clear from my interaction with people all over the world that few non-Jews actually understand very much about Jesus' Messiahship. Since Jesus did not come to start a new religion (i.e., the Christian faith), even though many Christians believe that Jesus came to do exactly that, if we are to understand the Bible correctly, we have to relate all of it to the plan that God had revealed in the OT (i.e., Old Testament). The OT is not simply a prelude to the NT (i.e., New Testament); it is its foundation. The NT cannot stand or be properly understood apart from the OT.

Jesus was sent by the Father to put in place everything needed for the fulfillment of the covenants that God had already promised to Abraham and to his descendants through Isaac.[1] So, Jesus came to fulfill the *Abrahamic Covenant*, giving the *Promised*

---

[1] Gen. 15:7-8, 13-14, 18; 17:1-8, 18-19; 25:22-23; 26:1-5; 27:28-29, 37; 28:13-17; Rom. 9:6-13.

Land to Abraham's seed through Isaac and Jacob;[1] He came to rule on David's throne in Jerusalem over the nation of Israel (and through Israel over the whole world), fulfilling the *Davidic Covenant*;[2] He came to lay the foundation for the fulfillment of the *New Covenant* for Israel by dying on the cross;[3] He came to give everlasting peace to the nation of Israel through His rule upon David's throne in Jerusalem, fulfilling the *Peace Covenant*.[4] All of these covenants are *everlasting* (which basically means *as long as this present earth lasts*) and involve the nation of Israel. Hence, all of the work of Messiah will involve or be connected to the nation of Israel in some way.

These major, Biblical covenants outline the direction that we should expect the history of the world to go. Israel's land is a divine promise and must be fulfilled; Israel's coming King is a divine promise and must be fulfilled; Israel's transformation spiritually is a divine promise and must be realized before the history of mankind can be concluded. Peace will be divinely se-cured for the apple of God's eye, Israel. *Jesus is first and foremost Israel's Messiah who has come to save the entire world in the way that the OT had predicted that salvation to occur, and only in that way.* Jesus did not come to save Israel, or anyone else, from hell and deliver them into heaven.

This is no small point so we must be clear on it.

When God began the process of moving toward the creation of the Church, the Body of Christ, upon this earth at Pente-cost in Acts two, *the message centered upon Jesus as the Christ or*

---

[1] Gen. 13:14-17; 15:7, 8-21; 17:8; and especially Gal. 3:15-19.
[2] 2Sam. 7:12-16; Psalm 89.
[3] Jer. 31:27-34. Cf., Lk. 22:20.
[4] Ezek. 34:11-31, esp. vv. 24-25.

Messiah of God (Acts 2:31, 36, 38). This is the message that Peter, the lead apostle of Jesus, first preached at that festival *after* Jesus' death, resurrection, and ascension.

That Jesus is the Christ (or Messiah) is the message that Peter and John preached in the Temple in Acts three and four probably within a year or so *after* Jesus' ascension (Acts 3:6, 16, 18, 20).

That Jesus is the Christ (or Messiah) is the message that Saul preached immediately after he believed in Jesus in Acts nine (Acts 9:20, 22). Here too Saul makes it clear that the title Son of God is a Messianic title. While he was not the first to equate these two titles (i.e., Messiah and Son of God),[1] it is notable that he communicates this truth to Luke, who writes the book of Acts, over twenty-five years after Jesus' earthly ministry. It is unnecessary, and most likely unbiblical, to make the phrase Son of God a reference to Jesus' divinity. This is not to deny in any way Jesus' divinity. But it is not founded upon the use of that title, but rather upon direct declarations of the Scriptures.

A coming Messiah was gradually revealed to Israel throughout the nation's history recorded in the OT. *Belief in Jesus is simply a continuation of that OT faith* (Lk. 1:46-55, 68-75). Both Zachariah the priest and Mary the mother of Jesus connect Jesus to the salvation that is promised in the OT, a deliverance "from our enemies and from the hand of all who hate us."[2] Because personal, practical righteousness is the condition for *that* salvation, Jesus' "salvation from sins" fits in

---

[1] Cf., John 1:35-41 to John 20:31. See also Lk. 4:41.
[2] Lk. 1:71.

beautifully with God's promise and man's expectation.[1] That is the reason that both Jesus and John the Baptist came preaching *repentance for the kingdom of heaven, the Messianic Kingdom, is near*. But this forgiveness is not at all related to obtaining heaven or escaping hell. It is related to becoming righteous in one's lifestyle so that the kingdom could be entered whenever it is established.

There is only one revealed faith in the entire Bible (Eph. 4:5).

One faith from beginning to end. One faith drawn out in the two Testaments. One faith progressively described in the OT, and culminated in the NT.

Consequently, the NT does not reveal a faith that *replaces* the OT faith. In the nature of the case, it cannot do that.

Rather, the NT faith fulfills and expands upon that OT faith (John 5:24; 12:44; notice that it was to the God of the OT that Jesus pointed all).

The NT does not reveal a different *salvation* from the one promised at the hands of Israel's coming Messiah in the OT. The individual salvation that is described in the NT is God's grace to man to achieve the righteousness that is required for entrance into Messiah's kingdom. NT salvation does not guarantee a heavenly destination or an escape from a fiery one.

It is striking, as you have already discovered in volume two of this series, that Saul repeatedly said that his belief in Jesus did not change what he had believed before he had come to faith in

---

[1] Matt. 1:21.

Jesus. Saul was *not converted* to a new faith; he was *further instructed* in the Jewish faith that he had already been grounded in as a child and as a Pharisee later in life. Saul, before he ever trusted in Jesus as his Messiah, was fully acceptable to God as every other OT saint had been. He was *in the faith* already. But he needed to receive God's new revelations concerning that faith. When he did, he became the most effective and usable disciple of Jesus among all the apostles.

According to the traditional dating of the books of the NT, one of the last books to be written was *The Gospel according to John the Apostle*. In John's purpose statement, given in chapter twenty, verse thirty-one, he continued to invite his readers around A.D. 90, some fifty-seven years after Jesus died, to *believe in Jesus as the Messiah, the Son of God*, in order to have life in His name. *Demonstrating that Jesus was the Messiah was still the message of John's gospel*, the last living apostle of Jesus.[1]

We must not underestimate the importance of John's overall purpose statement: believing that Jesus is *the Christ, the Son of God*. The Father never intended for faith in His Son to remove a person from the faith that he had already placed in Him, the God of all creation, the sustainer of all life, and the God of Israel. God never intended anyone to think that believing in Jesus took him beyond the OT faith, generally speaking.

And *the life* that Jesus would give to the one who believed in Him? It was *an abundant life*, a life that could be experienced in degrees throughout the rest of man's history upon planet earth. *This life* is, most probably, *directly connected to the age to come*, the coming Messianic rule upon this earth in fulfillment of the inviolateable covenants mentioned earlier. And, as such, *this life* will

---

[1] John 20:31.

16

be connected to the life experienced under the New Covenant of Jeremiah chapter thirty-one. But for now, *this life* is only "a taste of the age to come" and not the complete experience of it.

We are not living in the *last age* even though we may be living in the *last days*. There is a wonderful age to come, but it does not dawn until Jesus the Messiah returns to earth to set that age up and rule over it. *Jesus did not come to primarily make you "fit" for heaven; He came to make you "fit" for the kingdom that He is going to set up on this earth for one thousand years.* After which the end of human history upon this earth will come.

All this being true, it is time to embrace the fact that *Christians are actually proselytes to the Jewish faith.* That faith is a belief system revealed by God and inscripturated by men who were born along by the Holy Spirit when they wrote, resulting in an inerrant and infallible record of God's will. To think that it is a Christian's duty to try to convert a Jewish person (or anyone else for that matter) to Christianity is to turn the Bible on its head.

There are *no conversions* in the OT in the sense that we use that term today. There are no Edomites who become Jews; there are no Moabites who become Jews; there are no Philistines who become Jews. After Israel's successful wars against her neighbors, there was no attempt to *spiritually convert* any of those defeated foes to Israel's faith in God. Even Jonah's preaching to the Assyrians, contained in the Book of Jonah, did not produce *conversions* though it did produce *repentance and faith toward God.*[1] It is interesting that, apparently, God had made Himself known to both nations although they had characterized and worshipped Him differently. This situation is worth more thought.

We've turned the message of the Bible on its head for many

---

[1] Jonah 3:5-10.

reasons, but none so seemingly benign as trying to make its *good news* more relevant to Gentiles, to people like you and me, by diminishing or denying Israel's future place in God's plan for planet earth. In our attempts to make the message applicable, we've changed the message entirely. We can't throw stones at anyone on this matter because we've all done that, unconsciously and unwittingly perhaps, but we have done it as we attempted to minister to someone that God had brought into our lives and who needed spiritual counsel. This inadvertent change of the Bible's message is unfortunate, and would be disastrous if it was not for the greatness of our God who can turn our most feeble attempts to minister into usable testimonies of His glory and grace.

I remember in my earliest days of ministry I changed the message of a passage because I had been misled about it. I was using a Scripture memory system that presented Bible verses under various topics so they could be learned and memorized more easily. I remember memorizing Matt. 18:19-20 as divine promises related to my personal prayer life. Those verses read as follows:

> "Again I say to you, that if two of you agree on earth about anything that they may ask, it shall be done for them by My Father who is in heaven. For where two or three have gathered together in My name, there I am in their midst."

About a year or two after I had memorized those verses and had taught them as encouragements to pray, a seminary professor pointed out to me that the context is not about prayer at all. The context is about disciplining church members for offenses done toward other members in the church. I was flabbergasted. I certainly did not intentionally misuse the verses to lead anyone astray. But I had misused them, and I had misled others nonetheless. I was doing the best I knew how at the time. But God wanted me to grow in my knowledge and in my handling of His Word. I'm still on that same path today.

It is so easy to repeat the mistakes of others. Each time we are taught a mistaken view of a passage, and we don't know any better, we pass that mistaken view on to others over and over again. Since we all do it, we must be careful not to become condescending when we observe other's doing it. God gives us a command to approach the study of the Bible as a hard-working laborer.[1] And then He warns all of us not to teach before we know that we have the message correct. If we do teach error, we will incur a stricter judgment.[2] And some errors are vastly more devastating to a person's spiritual life than others.[3]

Jesus is the Messiah.[4] That is the central focus of the message of the entire NT even though it is not all of that message. He is the Jewish nation's Messiah, and He is your Messiah if you have believed in Him even though you may not be Jewish.[5] And as God's Messiah, He came to fulfill God's promises and covenants to Israel. *None of His work can be rightly understood if it is detached from His Messiahship.*

The Church does not replace Israel, and it can in no way become the recipient of the promises and covenants given to Israel. Either God becomes a liar who is unfaithful to His promises, or Jesus is a part of God's plan to bless Israel by fulfilling those promises so that Israel can become a blessing to the rest of the world. *Since those promises and covenants have nothing to do with*

---

[1] 2Tim. 2:15.
[2] James 3:1.
[3] 2Tim. 2:16-18; Tit. 1:10-11.
[4] John 4:41-42 (check v. 42 in Hodges'-Farstad's Greek New Testament).
[5] John 1:35-41; 4:22, 25-26; 20:31.

heaven, Jesus didn't come to spiritually save anyone into heaven. He came to save you from your sins and the world's defilements as you walk by faith, experiencing His supernatural life. And *that on-going salvation* will assure you of the salvation that is coming when Jesus returns to earth.

That Jesus was preached as the Messiah, the Son of God, is not to be debated. It is a fact. Next we must look at a few of those prophecies identifying the Messiah. Fulfilling those prophecies prove that Jesus was the promised Messiah, and give us some of those reasons that He was identified and preached as Israel's Messiah. No one else can make a claim to that office because no one else can fulfill what He alone has fulfilled.

Chapter 2

Fulfilled Prophecies Require It

Every year high school athletes hope to be recruited by a power five, college football conference. And each year juniors and seniors from the college ranks hope to be drafted by a professional football team which is a member of the National Football League. There are certain *measurables* that college football coaches look for before they extend their scholarship offers to graduating high school seniors. These are the same *measurables* that the professional coaches evaluate before a particular college athlete is considered worthy enough to be drafted by an NFL team. These *measurables* include such things as height, weight, length of arms, quickness, speed, strength, and performance on the field. All of these characteristics can be measured. All of them are very objective. They exist right before your eyes.

While there may be other, more intangible, attributes that should be considered, many coaches have little success in evaluating those subjective traits. As a result, they stick with the obvious, visible *measurables*. Some of these intangible attributes are leadership, determination, play-making or quick decision-making abilities when plays break down, poise, and confidence. Sometimes even though a player doesn't possess all of the *measurable* attributes, like having the desired height, weight, speed, length of arms, quickness of feet, and so on that are expected of an athlete to be successful, college and professional coaches may still take a chance on him because of his intangibles. These are especially impressive to coaches if they consistently put the athlete that possesses them within reach of victory.

And, of course, the biggest intangible of all is what is called the "it" factor. The "it" factor is that intangible that is exuded from a player with extremely special gifts of leadership, poise, confidence, and success on the field of play. The player with the "it" factor simply seems unstoppable. He rallies other players to play their best and to keep playing their best even when they are behind in a tough ball game. He somehow elevates the play of all those around him. He is not only a leader but a winner as well. Though it is an intangible attribute, there is just something special about the person who possesses the "it" factor.

If the intangible attributes are present and the typical external *measurables* aren't, many coaches, who don't trust the intangibles that they can't measure, depend only on what they can see. As a result, these coaches end up not giving some really good players a chance to show what they can do even though they have both the heart of a champion and success on the field. But for these coaches, they don't have enough of the external, visible *measurables* to be recruited.

There are both *measurables* and *intangibles* that ought to lead people to trust in Jesus as the Jewish Messiah. When considering only what Jesus had taught and not also what He had done to authoritatively verify that what He had taught was from God, many people have drawn the wrong conclusion about Jesus' identity. if the fulfilled prophecies are added, the decision is placed well beyond a doubt. Like anyone in any endeavor, when only part of the evidence is considered, the likelihood of drawing the wrong conclusion is greatly heightened. C.S. Lewis once addressed this situation when he said,

"I am trying here to prevent anyone saying the really foolish thing

22

that people often say about Him [i.c. Jesus]: I'm ready to accept Jesus as a great moral teacher, but I don't accept his claim to be God. That is the one thing we must not say. A man who was merely a man and said the sort of things Jesus said would not be a great moral teacher. He would either be a lunatic — on the level with the man who says he is a poached egg — or else he would be the Devil of Hell. You must make your choice. Either this man was, and is, the Son of God, or else a madman or something worse. You can shut him up for a fool, you can spit at him and kill him as a demon, or you can fall at his feet and call him Lord and God, but let us not come with any patronizing nonsense about his being a great human teacher. He has not left that open to us. He did not intend to."[1]

Jesus had both *measurables* and *intangibles* which I would like to present to you in the next two chapters. But I want to do that simply. When I first went into Christian ministry, I was trained in basic evangelism and basic discipleship. I remember being taught the K.I.S.S. method in both disciplines: *K*eep *I*t *S*imple, *S*tupid. Over the years whenever I veered from that method, the results were far less encouraging than when I kept to it.

Most people want to know the truth without all the details and rationales underlying the truth being given. The temptation to be *heady*, to be profound, so that I could be *complete* in my presentation, was ever before me. But most preferred the truth to be simply delivered so that it could be readily understood, used, and passed on to others.

There will always be the need for those who can set before others all the reasons for a certain position, yet the majority of people that I have ministered to over the years have not required all of those proofs. They seemed almost intuitively to recognize the truth that was being presented to them. I suppose

---

[1] Lewis, C.S. (Clive Staples), *Mere Christianity*, revised edition, New York, Macmillan/Collier, 1952, p. 55 ff.

this was due to the convicting work of the Holy Spirit.[1]

In keeping with the K.I.S.S. method then, I will present just six simple prophecies that should narrow the list of possible candidates for Messiah down to just One. These prophecies are not vague or hidden somehow in the Bible so that the reader needs a code of some sort to finally discover and properly interpret them. These are well-recognized prophecies by both Jewish and Christian students of the Bible. Let's see where they lead us, shall we?

A Man

The first prophecy that I want to focus upon is given in Gen. 3:15. God is speaking to the serpent in this verse and says,

> "And I will put enmity between you and the woman,
> And between your seed and her seed;
> *He* shall bruise you on the head,
> And you shall bruise *Him* on the heel."

While there is indeed mystery here, one thing seems clear: God is going to provide through the woman *a seed* who will bruise (or crush) Satan on the head while Satan is allowed to bruise (or crush) *Him* on *His* heel. This seed is identified as "a man" by the personal pronoun *he* and the masculine singular suffix for *him* that are used. Consequently, the promised seed of the woman will be a man, and not a woman.

The person God promised to send through the woman will be, in some way, the answer to all of the problems created by each person's first sin. The Promised One will be God's answer to man's *spiritual death*, a problem related to this life alone. He will also be God's answer to man's *personal sins* (like the disobe-

---

[1] John 16:7-11.

dience of Adam and Eve in eating the forbidden fruit), to man's opponent, *Satan* (who could easily overcome man at any time except for God's intervention prohibiting this), and to man's *change in constitution* resulting from his first sin. With man's first sin, he gains something in his constitution that he did not have before, something that the apostle Paul calls *indwelling sin* in Rom. 7:17, 20.[1] Being *a part of his human nature*, this entity, called indwelling sin, must remain with man as long as he continues to be man, that is, a human being. While indwelling sin is only a part of man's human nature, it is inseparable from the rest of his nature. The Promised One, when He comes, will deal with all of these issues successfully in some way. These issues have been addressed in volume four of this series, *Freedom through the Cross.*

From the NT we discover that God intended the death of the Promised One to be the means for providing man with the solutions to the problems he created by sinning. God took care of these things for all men everywhere. *The solution is universally applied to all men* since the problems repeatedly arise when each person sins his first sin. Faith is never declared to be the condition for the application of the cross to solve these needs. Rather, God solves them all by the gracious provision of His Son's death on the cross.

God's promise to send *a man* cuts out about 50% of the human population. While that is a significant observation, it might not be very impressive to some. So, let's continue.

---

[1] Theologians like to refer to this as a sin nature. But since that phrase is *never* used in the Bible and since it almost assuredly leads the user of it to wrong conclusions (e.g., that man is totally depraved), it is best to adhere to the various descriptions or labels the Bible does use for it.

From the Line of Abraham

It is important to understand that the coming Messiah would be from the line of Abraham. So important is this fact that the NT opens up with this pronouncement in the very first verse in *The Gospel according to Matthew*:

> "The book of the genealogy of Jesus Christ, the son of David, the son of Abraham." (Matt. 1:1)

This verse confirms the fact that the Christ, or Messiah, would be from the line of Abraham even though it does not tell us the reason this descendancy is so important. A correct understanding of the OT could have done that, however. To be of Abraham's choice seed is to be identified as the guaranteed inheritor of the Promised Land. *The Book of Galatians* explains to us that Jesus was the promised seed[1] to whom the Promised Land, guaranteed by the Abrahamic covenant,[2] was to go. *Jesus alone, then, is the Promised Heir of the Promised Land.* Ultimately, it appears, the Promised Land is not the possession of any nation *per se.* It was to be held in escrow by a certain part of Abraham's lineage until the ultimate Inheritor, sent by God, should come.

So, the Promised Land is the guaranteed inheritance of the Messiah who, in turn, is the Promised Savior and King of Israel.[3] He will obtain the land and then distribute it to the twelve tribes of Israel so that they can possess it and live on it unmolested.[4] If a person within the nation of Israel is not properly related to Him,[5] when he has a chance to be related to Him, that person will not be included in the enjoyment of the time of fulfillment

---

[1] Gal. 3:16.

[2] Ps. 105:8-11.

[3] John 4:22; Rom. 11:25-26.

[4] Ezek. 34:11-31. This will fulfill God's Peace Covenant to Israel.

[5] Gal. 3:26-29.

of this covenantal promise nor in all the blessings that accompany its fulfillment.

It should be obvious now how much the list of potential candidates for Messiah has been cut down. No one outside the line of Abraham could qualify. Since no one outside the line of Abraham should be given a second thought, Matthew only takes Jesus' genealogy back to Abraham.[1]

From the Tribe of Judah

The next prophecy, in our selection of six, that we find as we move forward through the Scriptures is found in Gen. 49:10. Jacob, inspired by God, is blessing his sons and telling them what will be true of them in the days to come. He does this for all twelve of his sons. When he comes to Judah, he says of him,

> "*The scepter* shall not depart from Judah,
> Nor *the ruler's staff* from between his feet
> Until *Shiloh* comes,
> And *to Him* shall be the obedience of the peoples."

This is not a phenomenon with which any of us in the West is familiar. Fathers don't prophesy over their children about their futures. Much less do fathers do this when they are on their death-beds. But that is exactly what is taking place here. We are not told how Jacob knew these things about his sons.

Jacob is predicting that the scepter belonging to a promised King would not depart from the tribe of Judah until that King comes and rules over all the peoples (of the earth). The promised Messiah would be a King over all Israel as He exercised rule over the rest of the world at the same time. While many kings

---

[1] Matt. 1:1.

would arise from Abraham's seed,[1] one of those kings would be the King of Kings, and the Lord of Lords. This one will be born king,[2] will be recognized as a king,[3] and will die because He declared Himself to be the promised King.[4] And when He returns, upon His robe and upon His thigh will be written the name King of Kings and Lord of Lords.[5]

So, with just three prophecies the line from which the Messiah would come has narrowed quite a bit. Now we know that He will be *a man* who is descended from Abraham and who must come from *the tribe of Judah*. Of the twelve tribes of the sons of Jacob, only Judah is the tribe of the prophesied King of Israel. And since each tribe was made up of a lot of families, it is possible to narrow down the list of candidates still further.

From the Family of David

The king that had been promised remained a somewhat shadowy figure until the time of King David who reigned from about 1010 B.C. to 970 B.C. After that time, Solomon took David's place *on David's throne* as the Messiah will do at a much later point in time in the history of mankind. The author of the book of Second Samuel clearly reveals to his reader that God chose David because of his spiritual walk with Him as the recipient of a kingly blessing. David would have a descendant who would follow him as king and who would have a spectacular reign of His own over all of Israel just like David, his forefather,

---

[1] Gen. 17:6.
[2] Matt. 2:2.
[3] John 6:15; 18:33-37. Cf., Mk. 15:18.
[4] Matt. 27:37; Mk. 15:2, 26; Lk. 23:38; John 19:19-22.
[5] Rev. 19:16.

had exercised. His rulership, once begun, would never come to an end. Through it God would fulfill all of the promises He had made to Abraham about the Promised Land and to David about his kingdom continuing over Israel. This coming king who would establish Israel as an independent kingdom on its own land would be a repeated motif alluded to by future prophets.

From Moses we learn that the Messiah would be a king as well as a prophet.[1] Moses did not know the family from which the promised King would arise even though he did know the tribe from which He had to come. Not until Samuel's contemporary writes the books known in the Western World as *First and Second Samuel*, about four hundred years after Moses died, does anyone learn that the King must come from the house and family of King David.[2]

While the context of 2Sam. 7:16 may be difficult and may be taken in more than one way since it refers to both Solomon and to a distant Seed of David that is left for the most part unexplained, Lk. 1:31-33 justifies the understanding being presented here. In that passage the angel Gabriel appears to Mary and promises her that the son she will bear will fulfill all the elements of the promise God gave to David. Gabriel explained it to her this way:

> "And behold, you will conceive in your womb and bear a son, and you shall name Him Jesus. He will be great and will be called the Son of the Most High, and the Lord God will give Him the *throne* of His father David; and He will reign over *the house* of Jacob *forever*, and His *kingdom* will have no end."

So, while Solomon might fit the description given in 2Sam. 7:12-15, verse sixteen explains that Jesus is the ultimate fulfillment of

---

[1] Gen. 49:10; Deut. 18:18-19.
[2] Lk. 2:4; 2Sam. 7:16.

the covenant God made with David. In light of other prophecies declaring a *vacancy* to the throne of David,[1] Solomon can't be the ultimate fulfillment of the divine covenant given to David. One must come after Solomon to rule over *the house of Jacob*[2] and the world[3] *forever*.[4] The term *forever* is not equivalent to our English term eternal in any way whatever. As we allow the Scriptures to interpret the Scriptures, we find that when *eternal* refers to the Messiah's promised Kingdom, it designates a 1,000 years reign.[5]

Consequently, Messiah's *eternal* kingdom[6] will have a beginning[7] and an end.[8] As the *Book of Daniel* makes perfectly clear, Messiah's kingdom, like the four kingdoms mentioned before His, is an earthly kingdom.[9] It ends when the earth upon which it is established is destroyed by God.[10] When the Bible is interpreted literally, it is impossible to construe the kingdom that Jesus offered as a spiritual reality without a physical presence.

Born in Bethlehem of Judea

The religious leaders were responsible for instructing the rest of the nation in the Scriptures. One of the prophecies known in the first century by apparently all the religious leaders of Israel was the identification of the birthplace of the coming Messiah.

Micah was the first prophet to reveal the birthplace of Messiah. As a result, no one prior to Micah's ministry[11] could have

---

[1] Hos. 3:4-5.
[2] Isa. 9:6-7.
[3] Zech. 14:9; Rev. 11:15. Cf., Isa. 24-27.
[4] Rev. 20:4-7.
[5] Cf., 2Pet. 1:11 to Rev. 20:4-7.
[6] 2Pet. 1:11.
[7] Matt. 25:31.
[8] Rev. 20:7-15; 1Cor. 15:23-28.
[9] Dan. 2; 7. See especially, Dan. 7:27.
[10] 2Pet. 3:7-13.
[11] Generally held to have taken place between 752 B.C. and 697 B.C.

known where the promised Messiah would be born. It simply had not been revealed by God before that time. Even Isaiah, who prophesied both the virgin birth and the propitiatory death of the Messiah, would have to learn from his contemporary the place the Messiah would be born.

When the Magi arrived in Jerusalem, they explained that they were seeking the young child who had been born *King of the Jews*.[1] After King Herod the Great sought them out, the religious leaders make it clear that the Messiah-King had to be born in Bethlehem according to the prophecy of Mic. 5:2 which said,

> "But as for you, Bethlehem Ephrathah, ... from you One will go forth for Me to be ruler in Israel."

This prophecy pinpoints the city in which the prophesied One had to be born, further narrowing the possibilities of those who could claim to be Israel's promised Messiah-King.

In general terms, the fulfillment of this prophecy is clearly said to be in *the days of Herod the King*.[2] Lest this dating be assumed to be gratuitous or even mistaken, it will be confirmed by prophecies from the Old Testament, given through the prophet Daniel nearly five hundred years earlier than Matthew's account.[3] The promised Messiah had to be born, had to live, and had to die at a specified time in history. Comparing Dan. 9:25 to Neh. 2:1-8 gives the time frame during which the Messiah had to come upon the scene, minister, and die (or to be *cut off* to use Daniel's euphemism that can be found widely used in the OT). And Jesus expected that time to be rightly calculated by the people living in the first century. He even rebuked the people in

---

[1] Matt. 2:2.
[2] Matt. 2:1.
[3] Dan. 9:24-27.

Jerusalem for not having recognized "the time of their visitation."[1] With great precision Sir Robert Anderson has calculated and confirmed these dates for us.[2] And this leads us to the sixth and final objective *measurable* that identifies the only person who can qualify as the promised Messiah from God.

The Time of Messiah's Coming and Rejection

When we take the information gleaned so far and add to it a prophesied date for Messiah's death, the field of possible candidates decreases to a very small field indeed. According to Daniel the prophet,[3] the Messiah had to be alive, presenting Himself as the promised One, four hundred and eighty-three lunar years after the decree by King Artaxerxes to restore and rebuild Jerusalem in 444 B.C.[4] There have been several suggestions that attempt to pinpoint the exact date alluded to here. The very best suggestions appear to differ from one another by only one to two years. Dr. Hoehner, a renown professor at Dallas Theological Seminary (and one that I was fortunate to have had in seminary), was highly respected by all who knew him for his care in collecting, collating, and interpreting the various facts related to this case. He has suggested that the date could be no later than A.D. 33, probably in March or April of that year.[5]

But whether the exact year is A.D. 31 or A.D. 32 or A.D. 33, the point is this: the promised Messiah could not come *after* that

---

[1] Lk. 19:44.

[2] Sir Robert Anderson, *The Coming Prince*, tenth edition. (Grand Rapids, MI: Kregel, 1957), pp. 88-105.

[3] Dan. 9:24-27.

[4] Neh. 2:1-20.

[5] See his book, *The Chronological Aspects of the Life of Christ*. (Grand Rapids, MI: Zondervan Publishing House, 1979), pp. 65-139. He accepts and follows Anderson's calculations.

date. He had to be already on the scene at this date because He was to be *cut off*, or killed, according to Daniel's prophecy, by that date.[1] Of course it is no coincidence that Jesus just happens to be crucified at this time in history. While the time of His birth was not specified in the Scriptures, the time of His death was.

Isaiah fifty-three explains what He would accomplish in His death. If that chapter were typed on a separate piece of paper and read to an audience, a gathering of either Israelis or Christians, or of anyone else who knew the details of the prophecies being discussed, that audience would overwhelmingly agree that the description being presented portrayed the death of Jesus Christ as accurately as a history written after the fact. But of course, Isa. 53 was written seven hundred years before the death of Christ, not before it.

And interestingly enough, this passage has always been left out of the Jewish yearly liturgy. Most probably it was omitted because it was so difficult to harmonize with the rest of the prophecies concerning the Messiah. How could the Messiah be both a Conquering King[2] and a Crucified Servant?[3] Both are prophesied so both must be true. The Jewish nation and many Christian institutions have responded to these issues by rejecting one (or manipulating its true meaning) and expounding the other.

The death of the Messiah and His resurrection are actually the great exclamation marks of the self-disclosure of God's Messiah. His death was predicted in the OT just as clearly as Jesus predicted His own death several times during His ministry. But included in His death predictions was a very short-termed

---

[1] Dan. 9:26.
[2] Zech. 9:9-10, 16; Micah 5:4-6; Isa. 9:7; etc.
[3] Isa. 52:13—53:12; Zech. 12:10; 13:1, 7; etc.

prophecy revealing the fact that His resurrection would occur just three days later. Through the resurrection, the Crucified Servant is enabled to become, at a later time, the Conquering King! Both are true. Both must be fulfilled. The Messiah would be a conquering King as well as a Crucified Servant. No one needs to choose one over the other. Both were prophesied. Both are helpful in identifying the promised Messiah.

The Conclusion Seems Apparent

When we piece together these six, simple prophecies, the list of candidates for Messiah dwindles, leaving really only one viable option: Jesus of Nazareth who must be the promised Messiah. He fulfilled these six prophecies which ought to be enough to satisfy even the most demanding investigator. It is true that He did not fulfill all of the prophecies that describe the Messiah's coming and the activities that He would accomplish when He came. But those prophecies that were left unfulfilled were all *conditional* in nature; their fulfillments were dependent upon the recipients to whom those blessing had been promised. If they had been righteous in their walk with God, these promises would have been fulfilled along with the rest.

A lack of preparation on the part of Israel,[1] even when faced with the Messiah's forerunner who heralded His coming and the need to repent,[2] was the reason that Jesus was unable to accomplish the rest of the prophecies that were predicted of the Messiah. Lacking practical righteousness in their lifestyles, the Jews could not enter the kingdom.[3] Consequently, the kingdom had to be delayed.

---

[1] Mk. 1:2-3.

[2] Matt. 3:2. Jesus had the same message (Matt. 4:17).

[3] Matt. 5:20.

Chapter 3
Jesus' Ministry Fulfills the Messianic Expectations

When I compared the obvious *measurables* that a football coach usually looks for in athletes to the prophetic *measurables* that Jesus fulfilled in His first advent, I was making the point that all the things that were visible, that could be readily seen, were enough to make most people realize that Jesus "fit the bill" as the promised Messiah. Now add to those prophecies that were fulfilled, the miraculous, compassionate ministry of Jesus toward everyone who crossed His path and His death and resurrection (touched upon in the next chapter but will be further developed in the following chapter), and you get the "it" factor.

The "it" factor, you will remember, is that attribute discussed in sports that designates an athlete as unique, a person who has it all. He is "the man!" The conclusion, that is naturally drawn when the prophetic *measurables* and Jesus' "it factors" are evaluated together, is that there is no reason to reject Him or to refuse to believe in Him. And this is exactly the conclusion that thousands of people in the first century drew even though many were afraid of the angry backlash of the religious leaders when they drew it.

Would we have been any different? Would we have had less fear over the possible consequences of believing in Jesus than those who had to deal with the angry religious leaders of the first century? I admit that I would have been tempted to keep my belief in Jesus a secret, just as many living in Jesus' day did, because of the fear of reprisal from the governing and religious powers that were rejecting Jesus.[1]

Everyone living at the time of Jesus' ministry recognized the power that was being displayed in it. Some openly declared His ministry had to be of God because of its supernatural nature. Others attributed His ministry to Satan who is, of course, God's supernatural adversary and the best *spin* that could be placed on the facts.[2] But generally speaking, whether a person was moved to believe in Him because of His miracles or whether a person was moved to reject Him even in the face of His miraculous signs, the conclusion that nearly all reached was *He did all things well.*[3]

When Nicodemus came to Jesus by night, he basically reveals to us what he already believed about this young teacher named Jesus. His comments to Jesus are recorded in John 3:2:

> *"**Rabbi**, we **know** that You have come **from God** as a teacher; for no one can do these signs that You do unless God is **with him**."*

Most of the time interpreters living in the twenty-first century find fault with Nicodemus (and with whatever faith he had) because he addressed Jesus as rabbi. Yet, if we can take a little clue from the woman at the well that Jesus interacts with in the fourth chapter of John's *Gospel*, it appears that it must have been a common belief that the Messiah, when He came, would tell His audience "all things."[4] In other words, He would be a master-teacher. Nicodemus might simply be referring to that teaching ability which the Messiah would possess when He announced to Israel all that God had given Him to say. So, rather

---

[1] Cf., John 9:18-23; 12:42-43; 19:38.
[2] See John 3:1-2 and Matt. 12:22-24, respectively.
[3] Mk. 7:37.
[4] John 4:25.

than being a slight, Nicodemus was actually holding forth the possibility that Jesus might be the Messiah when he called Him rabbi.

Also notice that Nicodemus, and those who had sent him on this little errand, *knew* certain things to be true about Jesus. There was no uncertainty in this part of their knowledge even though it involved God's calling of and God's work through another person, namely, Jesus. *The hand of God may often be invisible, but it remains nonetheless discernible for the spiritually sensitive.*[1]

Nicodemus already believed that Jesus had come *from God* and, furthermore, that God was *with Him still.* As it is true in many other places in the Scriptures, there is no discernible difference between Nicodemus' *knowledge* and his *faith* here.[2] Nicodemus' faith was based upon his observance of the miraculous deeds that Jesus was performing.[3]

This Pharisee was completely *correct* in his evaluation of what he was seeing. But it was not yet *precise.* What he saw led him to believe that Jesus was *from God* and was being used *by God.* But it did not yet lead him to believe that Jesus was the Messiah promised in the OT. He recognized Jesus as *a teacher* which could have led him easily enough to believe in Jesus as Messiah, but it could also lead him to believe that Jesus was either the coming prophet[4] or the expected teacher of righteousness.[5] The religious leaders at this time didn't know that all of

---

[1] This is the great lesson of *The Book of Esther*. Cf., also Rom. 1:19-20.

[2] It is common in *The Book of Acts* to read that faith or believing is a rational, persuasive phenomenon (e.g., Acts 17; 18; 28:23-24). Also the author to *The Book of Hebrews* gives us the closest thing to a definition of faith when he says that faith is a conviction (Heb. 11:1).

[3] Cf., John 2:23-25. This is the introduction to and the explanation of Nicodemus' initial comments to Jesus. It would have been better to have these verses begin chapter three than to have them end chapter two. The connection to chapter three is transparent.

[4] Deut. 18:16-18.

[5] Isa. 11; Hos. 10:12. The Qumran Community thought Messiah would be this person.

these roles would be fulfilled by the same person, *the Messiah* of God. But Nicodemus was about to make that move from teacher and prophet to Messiah as he spoke to Jesus about the promised kingdom of Messiah.

The man Himself, His teachings, and His miracles were too much for Nicodemus to explain away. Soon he would trust in Jesus as Messiah. Maybe before the night had ended.

Believing in the miracles of Jesus and believing in the person of Jesus as Messiah were positive responses to the light that God was giving through His Son. Both responses were evidences of a walk with God who was drawing a person into a more profound fellowship with Himself than had previously been experienced.

The purpose of the miracles was to establish the truth that Jesus had come from God as Messiah. Jesus explained the value of the miracles that He performed this way:

> "... 'do you say of Him, whom the Father sanctified and sent into the world, "You are blaspheming," because I said, "I am the Son of God?" If I do not do the works of My Father, do not believe Me; but if I do them, though you do not believe Me, *believe the works*, that you may *know* and *understand* that the Father is in Me, and I in the Father.'" (John 10:36-38, emphasis mine)

The miracles were performed for the purpose of testifying to the fact that Jesus was indeed *the Son of God*, that is, that He was the promised *Messiah*. Not only was Jesus sent *from God*, He was in a unique way the promised *Immanuel*.[1] He was "God with us" just as Matthew declared that He would be as He fulfilled the prophecy of Isa. 7:14. He was *in* the Father and the Father was *in* Him in a way that necessitated that He was the perfect representation of the Father and His will.[2]

---

[1] Matt. 1:23.
[2] Heb. 1:3; John 14:7-9.

It is, therefore, misleading to distinguish the God of the OT from Jesus in the NT. If Jesus is *the exact representation of the Father*, as Jesus Himself affirmed that He was, then *the God of the OT is exactly like Jesus of the NT*. To come to any other conclusion is to misunderstand the revelation that has been given to us. It is unfortunate that some of our doctrines about the nature of God and His work in salvation are so radically different from the Jesus described in the Gospels.

What Jesus *thought*, the Father was also thinking from His throne in the heavens since Jesus came to do the Father's will.[1] What Jesus *felt*, the Father was also feeling as He kept each person's tears in His bottle of remembrances.[2] What Jesus *did*, the Father would have done if He had acted independently of the Son that He had sent into the world to accomplish His will.[3] Jesus was the perfect representation of the Father because He was God Himself. He could only do what the Father would have done. He was called Immanuel, God *with* us, because He was God walking *among* us.[4] Yet, He and the Father are separate persons. A mystery to be sure. But the teaching of the Bible throughout.

Jesus submitted to and carried out the Father's will, having no will or words of His own.[5] And the miracles that He performed were *signs* pointing to these facts, facts that were to be received even if they could not be fully comprehended. In this case the evidence took people beyond the point that their minds were capable of understanding. Even the apostle Paul would say

---

[1] John 5:30.
[2] Ps. 56:8; Lam. 3:22-23, 31-32.
[3] Cf., John 5:36; 17:4; Heb. 10:7-14.
[4] Phil. 2:5-8; Heb. 1:3: John 20:28; John 1:1-5, 14; Col. 2:9-10.
[5] John 5:18-20, 30, 36.

almost thirty years later that these facts constitute the "mystery of godliness."[1]

When John the Baptist sent two of his disciples to Jesus in an attempt to confirm that He was indeed the Messiah, Jesus told the men to return to John, who was now in prison and close to death, and tell him what they had personally *heard* and had personally *seen* in Jesus' ministry, namely, that:

> "the blind receive sight and the lame walk, the lepers are cleansed and the deaf hear, and the dead are raised up, and the poor have the gospel preached to them." (Matt. 11:5)

Jesus did not give John's trusted disciples any new information to help them identify Him as the Messiah. He only asked them to draw their conclusions based upon what they *heard* Him teach and upon what they *saw* Him do. These observations, along with the specific *signs* that were given to John to help him identify the Messiah, namely, the voice of God the Father from heaven and a descending dove coming to rest upon Jesus at His baptism,[2] were all that God deemed necessary for John to draw the correct conclusion about Jesus' identity.

God repeatedly held each man, exposed to the ministry of Jesus, responsible to draw the correct conclusions from the information that was before him. He does the same thing today. The nature of the Messiah's ministry was clearly miraculous, one that could happen only if God Himself was *with Him*, supporting Jesus' ministry by His own supernatural power (generally made available through His Spirit). His works were intended to validate His words.[3] And if God had sent Jesus to declare His words, and if these words were rejected, God had warned

---

[1] 1 Tim. 3:16.
[2] John 1:32-34.
[3] Cf., e.g., John 10:37-38; Heb. 2:3-4.

that severe consequences would fall upon the rejecter.[1]

When Jesus listed the miracles that He was doing for John's messengers, He was referring to a revelation God had given to the prophet Isaiah about the land and the people of Israel. The context of that verse describes the time of the Messiah's coming. *In that day*, the wilderness and the desert will be glad, an euphemism for the renewal and revitalization of the land of Israel from Lebanon to the city of Jerusalem and on through to the Negev. *At that time* the glory of the Lord and the majesty of Israel's God will be seen by all. So, Isaiah prepared Israel for praise:

> "Encourage the exhausted, and strengthen the feeble. Say to those with anxious heart, 'Take courage, fear not. Behold, *your God* will come with vengeance; *The recompense of God* will come, But He will save you.' *Then* the eyes of the blind will be opened, and the ears of the deaf will be unstopped. *Then* the lame will leap like a deer, And the tongue of the dumb will shout for joy." (Isa. 35:3-6a)

While not all of Isaiah's prophecy was fulfilled in Jesus' ministry, those elements of it that Jesus referred to explicitly were. The *blind* were receiving their sight; the *deaf* were gaining their hearing; the *lame* were walking; and the *mutes* were enabled to speak. Obviously, these were significant miracles, performed repeatedly upon multitudes of persons. [2] To perform these deeds, as Nicodemus already rightly observed, God had to be with the man doing them.

In addition to the things Isaiah predicted would occur in the day that God's glory and majesty were seen in Israel, Jesus also performed other miracles as well. He healed the sick; He cast out demons; He even raised the dead. And He did these things to multitudes of people. In Jesus, God was certainly present among

---

[1] Deut. 18:16-19.
[2] Cf., Matt. 8:16-17; 9:35; 15:29-31.

His people, Israel, verifying Jesus' identity by the miracles that He performed for all to believe that He, and no one else, was the promised Messiah. God had used this tactic before; it was not a new approach by God to convince His people of His presence.[1]

When the reader studies the first four books of the NT, he is left with almost no alternative than to believe that Jesus was the prophesied Messiah. The overwhelming preponderance of the facts lead to that conclusion. He came to establish His identity by fulfilling the prophecies outlining Messiah's coming and describing the miraculous ministry Messiah would have. When a person rejects Jesus as Israel's promised Messiah, it is not done because of a lack of evidence, but because other issues have trumped the overwhelming evidence that has been given.

It is a terrifying reality that all the evidence that God chose to give to help a person identify the Messiah can be nullified by a person's *cultural background*. God expects each person to deal honestly with the evidence He has put in front of him. If that requires him to remove himself from associations that were previously supportive of him or from convictions that he had been developed over years of training, He expects that to take place. A willingness to objectively critique the evidence, compare it to all the cherished beliefs that have become a part of his convictions and conscience, and then draw the right conclusion is each person's responsibility before the Lord. *If we are spiritually dull in this process, it will result in our own undoing.*

---

[1] Ex. 4:1-31, especially verses 30 and 31. In this He could be likened to Moses.

Chapter 4

Jesus' Death and Resurrection
Prove His Messiahship

Back in 1993 I was diagnosed with cancer in my left kidney. I experienced an amazing relationship with the Lord during that period in my life. God used it to ground my trust in Him and to reveal His love and care for me at the same time. But beyond what trusting God through this trial did for me, my walk with the Lord through my ordeal impacted many others as well.

My point is *God usually does what He does to accomplish more than one purpose at a time.* He is awesome in that way! Not only did my experience benefit me; it also benefited those who watched me walk through this typically troubling and angst-producing trial with incomprehensible peace.

The same principle is at work in the death and resurrection of Jesus. God intended to use those momentous events to accomplish more than one goal and to teach more than one lesson. It is not a debatable issue that Jesus predicted His own death and resurrection. In fact, He did this numerous times. But, possibly, of even greater significance than the fact that He predicted His own death and resurrection is *the stated purpose* of these two events. While they accomplish a lot of things that are important for everyday living, they also help to verify that Jesus is the Messiah that God had promised in the OT Scriptures.

When Jesus began His fourth and last year of ministry, He began to predict His death and resurrection. The first revelation

43

to the apostles on these topics came in March of A.D. 32 just before His transfiguration.[1] And if you remember, Moses and Elijah appeared with Jesus on that mount and talked with Him about His *exodus* (or *departure*) from this earthly life.[2]

Within the following month, Jesus again broached the topic of His death and resurrection. And this time the text specifically states that *the apostles did not understand* what Jesus was talking about. But this was not entirely their fault since *they were being kept from understanding*[3] what was about to happen to Him.

Then just before His passion week, the last week before He would be put to death, He again explained to His apostles that He had to die and rise again. But apparently His closest disciples still did not grasp what He was predicting.[4] While there are at least six or seven other references about His death and resurrection that can be gleaned from Jesus' parables or passing comments,[5] these three expositions seem to be more focused, detailed, and central to what He was teaching them at the time. But the apostles remained in a deep fog concerning both of these coming events.

Now it must not escape our notice that *Jesus' apostles had received eternal life* (and are *incorrectly* considered to be saved based upon Acts 16:31 and Eph. 2:8-9) *even though none of them believed in His death or in His resurrection*. Their unbelief is a simple fact spelled out for us in the Gospels and should not be denied. *None of the salvations that Jesus offered is dependent upon believing in His death and resurrection.*

---

[1] Matt. 17:1-13; Mk. 9:2-4; Lk. 9:28-31.
[2] Lk. 9:31.
[3] Lk. 9:45.
[4] Lk. 18:34.
[5] Matt. 12:38-42; 20:18-19; Mk. 8:31-33; Lk. 13:22, 32-35; 17:25; John 2:18-22; etc.

Repeating the apostles' situation might be difficult, if not impossible, to do today since the death and resurrection of Jesus are part of *the gospel message* that is generally proclaimed at the outset by the person introducing Jesus to others. Nevertheless, care should be taken lest we make an assumption the rule of thumb rather than the demands of Scripture.

Although the apostle Paul never spelled out how the resurrection of Jesus proves His Messiahship in his thinking, he did state this connection rather plainly in Rom. 1:1-4:

> "Paul, a bond servant of Christ Jesus called an apostle, set apart for the gospel of God, which He promised beforehand through His prophets in the holy Scriptures, concerning **His Son**, who was born of a descendant of David according to the flesh, **who was declared the *Son of God* with power by the resurrection from the dead**, according to the Spirit of holiness, Jesus Christ our Lord…"

Because of the fairly consistent usages in the NT of the term *Son of God* to refer to the *Messiah*,[1] this verse declares Paul's conviction, based on God's revelations to him, that the phrase *His Son* is a reference to the *deity* of Jesus[2] (he was essentially God come in the flesh),[3] and the phrase *Son of God* is a reference to Jesus being the promised *Messiah*. This interpretation understands Paul to be referring to both the divinity of Jesus as well as the humanity of Jesus in his opening salutation to the churches in Rome, but distinguished these identities by these different phrases.

So, Jesus' Messiahship was powerfully set forth, Paul says, by His resurrection from the dead. Since Paul does not elucidate

---

[1] Cf., John 1:35-51; 20:31; Acts 9:20, 22; etc. The apostle John's use of the phrase *Son of God* as an appositive in his purpose statement ought to guide the interpreter in all the uses of the phrase, *the Son of God*, throughout his gospel narrative.

[2] Cf., Isa. 9:6.

[3] John 1:14; Col. 2:9; Phil. 2:5-8.

this comment for us, we should take care in how we interpret it. Maybe the best way to handle it is to understand Jesus' predictions of His death to be the interpretation we are seeking here. In each of His precisely focused and carefully worded predictions,[1] He declares that the Son of Man, which is, like the phrase Son of God, a Messianic title, must die and be raised on the third day. As a result, even if we have trouble articulating the precise reasoning Paul had in mind when he wrote Rom. 1:1-4, we can rest on the fact that since Jesus said that the Messiah, the Son of Man and Son of God, had to die and resurrect three days later, these events must be wrapped up in the work that He accomplished and in His identity as the Messiah.[2]

We know that the prophet Daniel gave us no alternative to the fact that the Messiah, the Prince who was prophesied to come, had to be *cut off*, a common euphemism for death in the OT. We also have passages describing the death of Messiah in Isaiah fifty-three and Psalm twenty-two. But the conviction that the Messiah must rise from the dead is a deduction which the Scriptures lead us to make.

Fulfilling all of the prophecies that were made concerning His death and resurrection, including those Jesus made Himself, might be considered the most demanding evidence of all that He was indeed the promised Messiah.

---

[1] Supra, pp. 29-30. Cf., also Matt. 16:16, 21; 17:22-23; 20:17-19.
[2] Certainly these events fulfilled the explicit OT Scriptures concerning Messiah's death and the implicit allusions (and the deductions springing from those allusions) concerning His resurrection (e.g., Ps. 16:10; Zech. 12:10; 13:7; etc.).

Section Two

Jesus Describes God and His Will

Chapter 5

Jesus Came to Explain God's Character

Many years ago my family was given an old Mercedes Benz. You read that correctly: we were *given* a 450 SEL Mercedes Benz. This was an unusual car in that, believe it or not, it was what we might call a lemon. I know! Who can imagine the words Mercedes Benz and lemon being used in the same sentence describing the same car? But the owner of this car had become so frustrated with the car that he let it sit for several years since it seemed to constantly require some new repair or some new part to keep it running. But to my family, we loved it because it was a gift from close, dear friends, who were trying to help us with our transportation needs.

On one particular occasion when I took the car in for a repair, a poster on the wall of this foreign car repair shop caught my eye. It said, "Wissen ist macht." Now a person doesn't need to know a lot of German to translate a short phrase like this. It is obvious from the English words that are easily associated with these German words that the translation would be something like "wisdom is might," or "knowledge is power." And even though the picture that illustrated the German slogan was a little risqué, it was exceedingly appropriate for a Mercedes Benz car repair shop.

I mean, really, who knows how to repair a Mercedes? You can't exactly drive it into your back yard, park it under a good shade tree, and repair it, right? Since I had to depend upon the knowledge of the men working in this repair shop, they had the power over me to charge whatever they thought was right. I had no idea of what was involved in any repair that they did to the car. And the price for repair? It was always an amount that took my breath away.

In Dan. 11:32b, a description of those living at a future time, even still future from our day, is given. The verse says,

"… but the people who do *know* their God shall *be strong and do* (mighty) *exploits*." (KJV)

At some future time in history when the world seems to be filled with deadly chaos and corrupt leaders tyrannizing so many of the nations, God's people, those who have a walk with Him in faith, will stand out, stand up, and overcome great odds even when it means their own death. Knowing who God is and what He is like will be the basis then, as it is the basis now, for *being strong and doing mighty exploits*. The knowledge of God is greater power than the knowledge of Mercedes Benz's car repairs.

About the same time that Daniel wrote his statement on the importance of knowing God, Jeremiah the prophet recorded this directive from God:

"Thus says the Lord, 'Let not a wise man boast of his wisdom, and let not a mighty man boast of his might, let not a rich man boast of his riches; but let him who boasts boast of this: that *he understands and knows Me*, that I am the Lord who exercises lovingkindness, justice, and righteousness on earth; for I delight in these things,' declares the Lord." (Jer. 9:23-24)

God wants to be known, and He wants to be known truly. Therefore, He has revealed Himself from the beginning of creation to the present time in all that He has made and in all that He continues to do in sustaining all that He has made.

God begins by declaring that He is a God who exercises lovingkindness. In fact, He wants to be known as that kind of God.

One entire Psalm[1] is dedicated to the praise of this particular attribute of God. No other virtue of God is extolled in any other psalm in a similar way. Even in times of terrible trials, it is this attribute that Jeremiah, the weeping prophet, focuses upon to maintain his hope. He wrote,

"This I recall to my mind, Therefore I have hope. The Lord's lovingkindnesses indeed never cease, For His compassions never fail. They are new every morning; Great is Thy faithfulness." (Lam. 3.21-23)

Consequently, it is no surprise then that the Book of Psalms singles out the lovingkindness of God as the basis for the praise of God.[2]

Next God wants to be known for His oversight of how man treats his fellow man and how He responds to all men. Since He is the Judge of the whole world,[3] righteousness and justice are the foundation of His throne on high,[4] and He makes this standard known to all men.[5] All men know a judgment is coming.

On the other hand, it has also been said that *a lack of the knowledge of God* is the root cause of every victory that wickedness has achieved. Voltaire, the French satirist, philosopher, dramatist, and historian who lived in the eighteenth century, is credited to have said,

"If God has made us in his image, we have returned the favor."[6]

For a self-acclaimed atheist, he certainly understood the basic dilemma of man. Because mankind in general has formed a

---

[1] Psalm 136. See also Ps. 107.
[2] Ps. 106:1.
[3] Gen. 18:25.
[4] Ps. 89:14; 97:2.
[5] Ps. 50:6-7; Rom. 1:20, 32; Micah 6:8.
[6] Retrieved on 6/4/16 from Wikipedia at https://en.wikiquote.org/wiki/Voltaire#Quotes.

mental picture of *a straw-god*, he is consumed with fears and doubts, uncertainties and turmoil. A.W. Tozer said,

> "We tend by a secret law of the soul to move toward our mental image of God."[1]

If we have imagined *a straw-god*, then he no longer is a strong tower to which the righteous can run for safety.[2] He turns into a broken down wall with an open gate behind which no safety can be offered and no help can be imagined.

If we have constructed *a straw-god*, then he is no longer our fortress or our shield[3] who can deliver from the snare of an enemy or from a deadly pestilence. Such a god cannot save from the ravages of man or from mayhem.

If we have constructed *a straw-god*, his way is no longer blameless in our minds for he is as frail as we are, and his strength can no longer make our feet like hinds' feet to set us in high places.[4] We have no greater help in him than in the best that a man can do.

But if the God that we imagine is the God of all creation, then His resources are unlimited. If He is the *only wise* God, His way cannot be improved upon. If He is the God of *love*, His way will meet our emotional needs as well as our physical and mental needs. If His throne is in the heavens, and if He *rules over all*, He can intervene instantly, if it is really best for Him to do that, or He can keep watch over us to ensure that the trial does not go beyond what we are able to endure while He supplies spiritually what we need to endure it.[5] We must remember that He knows

---

[1] A.W. Tozer, *The Knowledge of the Holy*, HarperCollins Publishers, p. 4.
[2] Ps. 61:3.
[3] Ps. 18:2; Ps. 91:2-3.
[4] Ps. 18:33; Hab. 3:19.
[5] 1Cor. 10:13.

our needs before we actually ask Him to meet them.[1] If He condemns humans for not meeting the needs of the less fortunate when they are able, He would be falling short of His own standard not to be ready to meet ours when we meet the conditions for His blessings.

We all struggle with our concept of God, and many of us are doing next to nothing to solve that problem. We don't move more closely to Him mostly because we don't realize how central our concept of God is to all of the issues, both disappointments as well as joys, that we face in life.

How can we *give thanks in all things* as the Scriptures instruct us to do[2] if we don't believe that He is good and that He is able to use even the evil actions against us for our good?[3]

How can we *rejoice always* or count every trial that comes our way a joyful opportunity[4] if we don't believe that He is present in the midst of our trials to sustain and to transform us as we experience His presence, His love, and His power?

Jesus taught His apostles that He not only came to explain the Father verbally, He also came to accomplish that goal by how He lived His life. So, the night before He was crucified, He said this to His closest disciples:

> "If you had known Me (as you could have), you would have known My Father also (much better than you do). . . . He who has seen Me has seen the Father . . ." (John 14:7, 9, parentheses mine)

Because Jesus was fully God, being essentially divine, while at the same time partaking of our human constitution, He perfectly illustrated how God the Father would have responded to all the

---

[1] Matt. 6:7-8.
[2] 1Thess. 5:18.
[3] Gen. 45:7; 50:20.
[4] Js. 1:2-4; 1Thess. 5:16; Rom. 8:35-37; 12:1-2.

situations in life that He (Jesus) was appointed to face. So, if we want to know what God is like, all we have to do is study the life of Jesus because He was God incarnate. He came to earth for the purpose of explaining the Father in word and in deed.[1]

So much is this the case that the author of the book of Hebrews says of Jesus,

> ". . . He (Jesus) is the radiance of His (the Father's) glory and the exact representation of His (the Father's) nature . . ." (Heb. 1:3a, parentheses mine)

Jesus' life was the effervescence of God's nature, exactly representing to us the Father in all that He was and did. How, I wonder, did Christianity end up with such a radically different view of God as is generally taught throughout Christendom? A god that *loves* some but not others; a god that *chooses* some (for heaven) but not all; a god that is so *condemning* that he sends the vast majority of people who have ever lived to *hell*; a god that offers *forgiveness* to some but not to all in the death of his Messiah; a god who must give *faith* for it to be present in the life of a person, and yet he gives it so sporadically that few become a spiritual well-spring for others. If Jesus represented the one true God as the Scriptures teach, then God must be entirely different from the god we have logically created in our theological treatises.[2]

There is a new book out. I was alerted to it by a friend who is studying the same soteriological issues that I am. The overall point of the book, which just happens to be represented in the title of the book, is a truth that is clearly stated several times in

---

[1] John 1:18.

[2] This paragraph needs a clarification. Many of the *italicized* terms above are used in the sense that they possess in traditional Christian theology. But this author has discovered that many of these meanings and referents are inadequate or incorrect altogether.

the Bible. I have never met a conservative Christian who did not believe the point this author discusses because it is a soundly Biblical fact. Consequently, it is my hope that it will achieve a wide-spread acceptance. The author portrays Jesus as *a mirror reflection of the invisible God*. In short, if we can develop and receive the concept of *a more Christ-like God*,[1] we can turn the world upside down. If Jesus beautifully represents the Father,[2] then the Father is exactly like Jesus!

If you have imagined that there was more than one god or that God's nature was different from what it actually is, those ideas are corrected by looking at and listening to Jesus. If you believe in multiple deities like the Athenians did in Acts 17, or if you believe in one god but you have attributed to your god a different nature than what God actually has, then you should realize Jesus is unique among all other people who have walked this earth (as the previous chapters have verified). Jesus was sent by the only true God to explain what He (God) is really like.[3]

God has continuously communicated with all men coming into the world what He is like and some aspects of His desired will for them. He has done this from the beginning of human history, using various means and various agents to accomplish His communication to man. But in these last days, He sent His unique Son in person to clarify His nature.[4] So He expects all men to *repent toward Him* and *have faith in His Son*[5] as they live their lives to the glory of the one, true God who is over all.

---

[1] That is the author's terminology which I just love! It is also the title of his book.
[2] Heb. 1:3; John 14:7-9.
[3] John 1:18.
[4] Heb. 1:1-3.
[5] Acts 20:21.

Since all men have built their very own *straw-god* to some extent (yes, you and I have done this too), we all need to retreat to Jesus to correct our view of God so that He can become the unperverted object of our faith that He desires to be. When we see Him as He really is, and when His will becomes the desire of our hearts, our faith will become unshakable.

Every person of every religion is being held responsible for correcting his view of God and returning to serve Him by trusting in Him as he lives out his life upon this earth according to God's revelation to him. So, the first thing that each person in the world needs to do is restudy the character of God, not just to get it right, but to enhance his spiritual life and to prepare himself for experiencing the blessings that a loving God has for him.

God dearly loves every person He has created and has provided through His unique Son, Jesus, an abundant life to be experienced right now in this life. But if a person refuses to make the adjustments that he needs to make, namely, to repent from how he has perceived God and from how he has dishonored Him, and to receive His Son for the life that He is offering, the heartaches and difficulties of life rest upon his shoulders alone. But when a person returns to God and develops a vital, daily faith in Jesus, then Jesus takes those burdens and offers him rest for his soul.[1]

While I cannot go much further into this discussion on the attributes of God in this forum, I can give you some tips to start you on your way to developing a right concept of God. Fortunately, I was first introduced to the importance of a right concept of God in my first year of ministry in 1970.

First I heard a message on Right Thinking by Dr. Earl Rad-

---

[1] Matt. 11:28-30.

macher. He challenged us with the fact that right thinking always begins with right thinking about God. The following summer this same speaker taught at a conference on various topics which included what the Scriptures declared concerning God's attributes (or character). It was such a challenging time that I could easily see the importance and relevance of this pursuit. He challenged us to begin studying this topic by means of every resource we could get our hands on. He asked the entire audience how many had even read a book on the character or attributes of God. No one raised his hand. Not one!

The first book I read on the attributes of God was A.W. Tozer's book, *The Knowledge of the Holy*. And to say that, for me, it was a life changer would be inadequate. I remember taking ninety-two pages of handwritten notes, mostly just copying down what the author had said that was so excellent, on a book that was only a hundred and seventeen pages in length! But with that book God began to come into focus for me.

While His greatness and majesty grew in my thinking, His involvement in my life, even His unseen hand and His ever-present attention to my circumstances, began to overwhelm me. Could I mean that much to God? Could He be that lovingly involved in my life? The knowledge of God became very powerful supporting for my entire being and ministry!

Then I read J.B. Phillips' book, *Your God Is Too Small*. It challenged me not to limit my concept of God to the proverbial clichés. Its approach is a psychological analysis of man's learned responses from early childhood through adolescence. While there is much truth in his examples, it is too subjective, too molded by human deductions (regardless of his dependence upon psychological "studies" that have been made), for it to provide a universal, unshakable foundation. But he does an excellent job of alerting a person to various possible distortions of God's character, regardless of how these distortions may have originated or how a person may have assimilated them.

One of the very best studies on the attributes of God has been written by Myrna Alexander. The title of her book is *Behold Your God, a woman's workshop on the attributes of God*. It is simply outstanding. I have used it with men with great success. The format of the book is very simple and easy to use. The author gives a couple of pages on each attribute, gleaned from the Scriptures, and then asks questions on each attribute, helping the reader to apply the information to his or her life. This is an outstanding tool for bringing a person closer to God if he/she maintains the faith responses in God suggested in the book.

And lastly, the book that has become my favorite was written by Stephen Charnock in 1664. The title of his book is *The Existence and Attributes of God*. While it is very difficult to read, it has the potential of creating the greatest life change of any book that I have read outside the Bible itself. But a caveat is required. When I first began reading the book, I could only read about a third of a page at a time. The book is over nine hundred pages long! It trained me to think while it gave me the content to think upon. I can safely say that probably no one reading this book has ever been exposed to a book of this sort. Books just aren't written this way anymore. But if you can get through it, it has the potential of transforming your life.

Knowledge is power. You can't trust God any further than you know Him. Get to know Him and get ready to do mighty exploits! That is the reason Jesus came to reveal His true nature.

Chapter 6

Jesus Came to Affirm God's Universal Will

Jesus came to do the will of the Father. In doing the will of the Father, He explained what God's will is and how one accomplishes it. Jesus emphasized these facts when He said,

> "I can do nothing on My own initiative. As I hear, I judge; and My judgment is just, because *I do not seek My own will, but the will of Him who sent Me.*" (John 5:30)

The responses that Jesus gave were communicated to Him from the Father. Whether it was an act that He was to perform or a teaching that He was to communicate,[1] He received the revelation of the Father's will from the Father and carried it out during His lifetime. So much is this the case that He could offer these words to the Father just before He was arrested, tried, beaten, and crucified:

> "I glorified You on the earth, having accomplished the work which You had given Me to do." (John 17:4)

Jesus was a person wholly devoted to performing the will of the Father throughout His entire life.[2]

Because of our programming, even though it may be considered orthodox in nature, we have accepted the unsupportable dictum that Jesus has changed the whole landscape, uprooting and discarding the old growth while planting entirely new seeds that change the scenery altogether. It appears to be quite inade-

---

[1] John 6:38-40; 7:16; 8:28-29.
[2] John 18:23.

quate to simply say that God has discarded the way He worked in the OT. Some of God's working principles seem to be quite universal in their application and permanent in their endurance.

The Gentiles in the OT did not possess the Laws given to Israel through Moses. Nevertheless, they could still be found to be righteous before God in their lifestyle. In this same way, the rest of the world do not need to believe in and to follow Jesus to be righteous before God. *The standard God put in place in the OT is the same standard that He still uses today.* But that standard does not fit with our orthodox theology.

God did not give the same full revelation of His will to every person under the sun *like He did to the nation of Israel.* That full revelation was gradually revealed to Israel, however. No generation had all of the revelation together until the last prophet had written around 433 B.C.

God gave each person *some* revelation for which he would be responsible. And if that person was obedient to the revelation that had been given to him, as he walked in faith, God would declare him righteous in his character and lifestyle. He did the same for the Jews when they obeyed the Law that He had given to them as long as they walked in faith as they performed it. Hence, the Jew who walked according to the Law in faith was righteous,[1] and the Gentile who walked in faith fulfilling the revelation that God had given him was righteous as well.[2] That standard has not changed today.

In the same way, God sent His unique Son into the world to give further revelation. But that further revelation only came to

---

[1] Ps. 1:1-6; Acts 13:38-39; Rom. 2:13; Lk. 1:6.

[2] Gen. 20:1-11. Notice that the term *blameless* in verse four is actually the term *righteous* (δικαιον) in the Septuagint, the Greek translation of the Hebrew OT. This situation was *before* the Law was given and *outside* the lineage God was mainly working with.

a relatively small segment of the world's population just like God's written revelation had done previously. Those who were given this new revelation are held to a higher standard than those who didn't receive it. No one can be justly held accountable for what he has not been given.[1] Just as the Gentiles were not held responsible for the Law given to the Jews in the OT,[2] the rest of the world is not being held responsible for the good news about Jesus until they are actually given that good news.[3]

Jesus *is* new revelation, and He *gave* new revelation during His ministry. To receive that new information and follow it would result in new blessings from God. But rejecting that revelation has the same consequence as rejecting any new revelation that God has ever given to man at any time throughout human history. There is incurred a loss of blessings and an estrangement from God in those particular areas about which God has made known new information. This principle is not a new truth. Isaiah set it forth over twenty-seven hundred years ago when he quoted God, saying,

> "For My *thoughts* are not your *thoughts*, Neither are your *ways* My *ways*, declares the Lord. For as the heavens are higher than the earth, So are My *ways* higher than your *ways*, And My *thoughts* than your *thoughts*." (Isa. 55:8-9, emphases mine)

Simply put, Isaiah was saying that no one can walk in God's ways apart from having His thoughts about the way in which he should walk. The assimilation of God's *thoughts* is necessary to walk in God's *ways*. So, to the extent that a person rejects God's thoughts, in this case His new revelation about and from Jesus, to that same extent that person cannot walk with God down the

---

[1] John 15:22; Rom. 10:14-15.
[2] Rom. 2:11-16; 3:29-30; 9:30-33; Gal. 3:8.
[3] Cf., Lk. 24:45-48; Acts 1:8; 8:26-38; 10:1–11:18; 17:22-23, 30-31.

path that He desires him to walk. But if he does refuse God's revelation about Jesus or about any other issue upon which God speaks to him, it does not follow that his whole life is, thereby, on the wrong path. *This all or nothing template that has dominated orthodox Christian teaching for so long is simply unbiblical.* While there may be found people who are heading toward that goal of knowing, believing, and following all that God has revealed to them, no one has ever reached it yet. And it is self-deluding to think otherwise.

Distinguishing between self-delusion and self-evaluation, it is time to take a quick look at how we have been accepting or refusing the new revelation that God is setting before us through this present series of books. At this point in our studies, we ought to have all come to the following conclusions if we are receiving God's Word as He desires us to do:

> *Justification* is about a person's *walk* with God, not his *stance* before God. Hence, justification is an aspect of sanctification, occurring daily, repeatedly, in the life of a person walking by faith. It has nothing to do with Christ's righteousness being *imputed*, in the sense of being *transferred*, to a person. In justification God declares the response that a man has given a righteous one if it was given in faith. Justification has nothing to do directly with the afterlife.

> *Salvation* is completely different from justification. The Bible never makes these two words synonyms. We have also learned that *salvation has nothing to do with heaven*, with going to heaven, or with an eternal destiny in heaven. *A person can be presently being saved and still go to hell.* Believ-

ing in Jesus doesn't guarantee a transport to heaven when he dies. Also, the Bible does not talk about a person being once-for-all-and-finally saved as though he has reached a standing or status before God that can't be changed.

The *righteousness* with which God is concerned is *practical* rather than *positional*. Practical righteousness is simply doing the right thing as one trusts in the intervention of God during the performance of the right thing. There is no positional righteousness that is connected to and that determines one's eternal destiny. No one needs a *perfect* righteousness to be acceptable to God or to go to heaven (at death) or to be qualified to be God's servant eternally.

Jesus' death did not secure anyone a place in heaven. What happens to a person in the afterlife is not connected to the cross since the cross only deals with this present life. *Forgiveness*, made possible by Jesus' death, is offered in connection to this life alone; it isn't applicable in the afterlife (or to a person's final judgment).

The cross makes it possible for God to forgive man's sins so that he can renew his fellowship with God day by day.

The cross overcomes man's slavery to indwelling sin so that the term *total depravity* should never have been used to describe man's condition as he walks upon this earth. The cross frees him to follow God *if he so chooses.*

The cross removes man from Satan's dominion, allowing him to choose whether he follows Satan or not.

These are just some of the revelations that we have discovered in our study up to this point. Now what a person does with these truths will impact his walk with God and his experience of God's blessings. They can be rejected; they can be accepted. Assuming that they are Biblical truths, man will be judged by God both now and in the life to come based upon his response to them. The judgment in the afterlife is according to what a person has done, not according to what he has believed or in whom he has believed.

The point in summary is this: *when God sent His Son to die on the cross and rise again, He did not change how a person finds acceptability with God in this life.* He did not create a new and exclusive way for the whole world to come to Him when He sent His unique Son into the world to die for it.

By the death of His Son on the cross, God historically provided *the basis that justified the way that He had been treating all men from the creation of the world.* The cross provided the propitiation that was needed for God to forgive any man at any time throughout human history. God had been relying upon the cross every time He accepted a sacrifice, or every time He received the repentant, or required baptism, or heard and accepted a person's confession of sin as the condition for that person to obtain forgiveness from Him. Through the cross God reconciled the world to Himself. That Jesus was slain before the foundation of the world allows God to be reconciled from that point forward. So, God stands on the porch, so to speak, with open arms waiting for His prodigals to return to Him.

As I explained in volume three of this series, while Jesus provides the way to God in the cross, God does not require a belief in Jesus for a person to take that pathway back to Himself.

Fellowship with God is a universal privilege (because of the cross). *Faith in Jesus is not.* If a person hasn't heard about Jesus, he can't believe on Jesus.[1] If he can't believe on Jesus, he can't partake of the privileges that come with that belief.

So, apart from faith in Jesus, who is new revelation and who gave new revelation, no one can have the new blessings that God is providing for walking successfully, spiritually speaking, in this present, evil age.[2] Believing in Jesus is the means of obtaining and using the new life that the Father wanted to give a person to help him live life successfully today.[3] How strange it is for people who have believed in Jesus to continue to walk like those who either have lived before Jesus came or like those who have rejected Him (i.e., in the power of their own strength).

What is the will of God for all men whether they live in the most privileged country in the world or in the most, apparently, God forsaken part of the world? *That will has not changed in over six thousand years of recorded Biblical history.* That fact alone is worth considering very deeply.

Beginning during the times of Abraham ~ which most researchers put between the twenty-third century B.C. and the beginning of the nineteenth century B.C., depending upon whether the Biblical guidelines are used or secular guidelines with their vast differences in dating assumptions and procedures[4] ~ we get a very general idea of what God required from man in Gen. 20:1-18. When Abraham was about one hundred years old, he traveled with his wife Sarah, who was ninety years old, to Gerar,

---

[1] Rom. 10:14-15.

[2] Acts 2:38-40; Gal. 1:4.

[3] John 10:9-10, 27-28.

[4] See Matt McClellan, *"Abraham and the Chronology of Ancient Mesopotamia,"* retrieved at https://assets.answersingenesis.org/doc/articles/pdfversions/Abraham_chronology_ancient_Mesopotamia.pdf on 1/16/16.

which was located west of Beersheba and southwest of Hebron near the Negev.

Here Abraham introduced Sarah as his sister rather than as his wife. The reason for this is explicitly given to us in the text. When examined by the King, Abraham confessed,

> "Because I thought, surely there is no *fear of God* in this place; and they will kill me because of my wife." (Gen. 20:11, emphasis mine)

Abraham assumed that there was no *fear of God* in Gerar. He was surprised, as many are still today, that there was a fear of God in that place and that fear, apparently, made an astounding impact upon the lives of the people. Not only is the entire nation described as *a righteous (or just) people*, but the King himself is described as a man of *integrity* of heart and *innocence* of hands.[1]

When God appeared to King Abimelech in his dream, there was no uncertainty as to which God this was that was appearing to him. Abimelech never doubted for a moment that this was the God to whom he was personally accountable. The God of Abraham was the God appearing to King Abimelech. And this God had impressed Himself upon this King and this nation so thoroughly that their lives had been constrained to live righteously or justly.[2] So in whatever way God had chosen to reveal Himself, the King and all the people of this nation knew the one, true God, and they knew Him even when there was no written revelation to explain Him (except possibly the book of Job).

These two qualities will be found throughout the Bible as the essential characteristics that God requires in any person for him to be acceptable to Him and blessed by Him: *Fearing God and do-*

---

[1] Gen. 20:4-6. Why would someone translate the term δικαιος as blameless when it *literally* means, as the marginal note admits, righteous (or just)? Theological exegesis?

[2] Cf., Ex. 20:18-20 which describe the nation of Israel six to eight hundred years later.

ing what is right. While these two qualities are described at times in slightly different, though understandably related, ways, they are the characteristics that evidence the presence of God and His hand in peoples' lives. This motif is found throughout the Bible and constitutes the universal will of God.

King Solomon is generally taken to be the wisest person that has ever lived on planet earth, besides Jesus of course. In his classic work on explaining life and what gives life its meaning and purpose, he summarized the entire message that he gave to Israel in *The Book of Ecclesiastes* in the last two verses. There he wrote these *universal truths for all mankind*:

> "The conclusion, when all has been heard, is: *fear God and keep His commandments*, because this applies to *every person*. For God will bring every act to judgment, everything which is hidden, whether it is good or evil." (Eccl. 12:13-14, emphasis mine)

Fear God and keep His commandments. These are the same conditions as fearing God and doing what is right because what is right is what God has communicated to a person He wants performed whether that person has the Mosaic Law containing the commandments of God, or he is without the Law of Moses altogether. After twelve hundred years, from the time of Abraham to the time of Solomon, the standard of God had not changed since it had been described in Abraham's encounter with King Abimelech. There are two qualities or characteristics that God still required for a man to find meaning and purpose in life and acceptability before Him. And to discover meaning and purpose may be one of the central drives or desires of every person who has ever lived.

Moving on another two hundred and fifty years or so, we come to the prophet Micah. Ministering around 750 B.C., he told the Southern Kingdom of Judah what kind of persons they must become to prevent God from bringing judgment upon them. This judgment included death for many and exile for the rest. What was it that God required? Micah spelled it out for every person when he said,

> "He (God) has told you, O man, what is good; And what does the Lord require of you but to do justice, to love kindness, and to walk humbly with your God?" (Mic. 6:8)

It did not matter if the person was in the line of the chosen people of God or not. Does this verse not perfectly describe Abimelech and his nation in Gen. 20:1-18? Does it not reiterate, though not verbatim, the conclusion that Solomon had come to after his long search for purpose and meaning in Eccl. 12:13-14? Abimelech and his people were outside the line of promise, outside the chosen people that God would use to receive and guard His revelation to man. Solomon, on the other hand, wrote to the chosen nation. But both messages are precisely the same: *fear God and do what is right*, and you will be acceptable to God and find meaning and purpose for your own life in your own circumstances! The standard is simple and reachable for all men living in all ages.

Did Jesus change this standard in any way during His earthly ministry? Did He add other requirements to the two essential characteristics that have been in place for over two thousand years of recorded, Biblical history? Did God's approach and message all of a sudden become exclusive? The exclusivity that orthodox Christianity claims for itself, a topic we covered in volume three of this series, has prevented many from seeing the world through God's eyes. Let's look into Jesus' ministry and into His discipleship message, especially to the apostle Peter, to test the validity of this claim to exclusivity.

68

In John 9:1-38 we have an excellent example of how Jesus ministered to people and the message that He preached and instilled into His disciples, one of whom recorded this episode for us. After Jesus healed a man who had been blind from birth, the religious leaders tried to manipulate the family and skew the message to explain away the miracle that had just taken place. In their attempted manipulation of the blind man, they declared, without giving any rationale at all for their pontification, that Jesus must be a sinner. The man responded,

> "'Whether He is a sinner, I do not know; one thing I do know, that, whereas I was blind, now I see.'" (John 9:25)

As their vindictive cross-examination continued, the blind man offered what appears to be a well-accepted axiom. He said,

> "We know that God does not hear sinners; but *if anyone is God-fearing* (having a reverential fear of or devotion to God)*, and does His will*, He hears him." (John 9:31, emphasis, parentheses mine)

There it is again! The same standard that has been in force for over the last two thousand years of recorded, Biblical history. What is God looking for? What does He require to answer the prayer of a man wherever he might be found? He is looking for a man who *fears Him and does His will.*

But wait! Aren't all of these examples *before the cross*? Don't they describe a standard that has now been changed *by the cross*? Even though the apostle John is writing to us *after the cross* when he describes the episode of Jesus healing the blind man, the assumption so often made is the cross changes everything.

It can be readily admitted that there are some changes that occurred at the cross. But those changes have been specified in the Scriptures. We must not *assume* that some standard changed if God has not *explicitly* declared that to be true. The last Biblical example, I want to set before you, establishes the fact that the standard of *fearing God and doing what is right* did not change in the slightest even *after the cross.*

Most Christians are familiar with the story of Peter's vision of the sheet coming down out of heaven with the unclean animals on it. God's voice comes out of heaven saying, "Kill and eat." That experience was ordained by God to motivate Peter to begin reevaluating his perspective on the people who live outside the chosen nation of Israel.

Peter didn't understand the meaning of the vision when it was first given to him. It was not until after he responded to God's next instructions to him that he understood it. In those follow up instructions, God told Peter to accompany strangers back to the home of a Roman centurion by the name of Cornelius.

As Peter was faithful to discharge the leading that God gave him, he himself would learn the meaning of the vision. He would become properly instructed in one area as he was instructing others in another area. No one should ever be tempted to think that because he possesses some truth in one area that he possesses all the truth in all other areas as well. The lesson Peter learned was a hard one as it is for every indoctrinated person.

Peter had formerly thought of Gentiles as "unclean" people, just like the unclean animals on the sheet that had come down out of heaven to him. But now God was telling him to go with the strangers who had come for him to a Gentile's home to preach Jesus to him. Peter was already shocked to hear Cornelius described in such glowing terms by the envoy that had been sent to invite him to Cornelius' home. They described Cornelius to Peter in this fashion:

"'Cornelius, a centurion, a *righteous* and *God fearing* man well spoken of by *the entire nation of the Jews*, was *divinely* directed by a holy angel to send for you to come to his house and hear a message from you.'" (Acts 10:22, emphases mine)

Once again we see those two essential qualities: *fear God and do what is right* (or be righteous or in right). These men's evaluation of Cornelius was surprising to Peter, but correct or accurately stated. God's own evaluation of Cornelius, given in verses one to four, proves this. Cornelius was *God-fearing*, and he was a *devout* and *righteous* man. For these reasons, God was responding to his prayers just as we should expect because of the truths given by the blind man in answer to the religious leaders' accusations in John 9:31.

But when Peter finally realized what God was trying to teach him, he took the truth he was learning a step further. Like Solomon did before him, *Peter universalizes the truth that God was teaching him at this time.* Peter said,

"'In truth I comprehend (now) that God is not one to show partially (to the Jews over the Gentiles), but in **every nation** the man who **fears Him** and **works righteousness** (does what is right) is received by (welcome or acceptable to) Him.'" (Acts 10:34-35, my translation, parentheses, and emphases)

Peter was saying that God would be partial if He had any other standard than these two essentials! All that He required from any man was to *fear Him and do what is right*. He was declaring for all times that men of *every nation* (and of every culture and of every religion) are welcomed to God if they have these two essential characteristics: *if they fear God and if they do what is right*. Re-read Peter's comments in Acts 10:34-35 if you find this hard to believe. It is only the theology that we have learned that is keeping us from the obvious meaning here.

71

It is God's responsibility to reveal Himself and to make that revelation clear to each man. He knows every man's capacity and exactly the best way to communicate with him. And since there is no one who can turn back the outstretched hand of God[1] or thwart His purpose,[2] His revelation must be sufficient, and it must be clear. As a result, the apostle Paul can say,

> "… that which is known about God is evident (or clear) within them; for God made it evident (or clear) to them." (Rom. 1:19, parentheses mine)

What God reveals is evident or clear because none other than He Himself is giving the revelation!

But a man can suppress the truth about God in unrighteousness and ungodliness.[3] He can take the clear revelation that God is giving and pervert it.[4] But in doing so, he is still without excuse before God[5] who will eventually turn him over to his own devices and bring judgment upon him.[6]

Peter's ministry to Cornelius occurred *after the cross*, establishing the fact that the standard that makes one acceptable to God is the same today as it was before the Old Testament had even been written. Jesus did not come to change this standard; He came to give a new life to make this standard more readily attainable in the chaotic world of the last days. The Bible does not allow us to draw the conclusion that Jesus came to start an entirely different religion. He came to enhance the faith in God that is described throughout the Jewish Scriptures.

---

[1] Cf., Isa. 43:13.
[2] Cf., Job 42:2.
[3] Rom. 1:18.
[4] Rom. 1:21-23.
[5] Rom. 1:20.
[6] Rom. 1:24-32.

In the same way that *loving God and loving your neighbor* fulfills all six hundred and thirteen commandments in the OT, *fearing God and doing what is right* fulfill the requirements for being acceptable in one's daily life before God. We are commanded to study God's word[1] and to meditate upon it[2] so that it can become a lamp to our feet and a light to our path.[3] This inscripturated revelation inerrantly and infallibly teaches us about God and about the specifics of His will. But if a person doesn't have that written revelation from God, he is responsible to obey the revelation that God has given to him. And it is reasonable to assume that the content of the Gentiles' unwritten revelation can be summarized in exactly the same way that Jesus summarized the Jews' written revelation: *love God and love your neighbor as yourself.*

---

[1] 2Tim. 2:15.

[2] Ps. 1:2.

[3] Ps. 119:105.

Section Three

Jesus Came to Redeem

Chapter 7

Jesus Came to Free Mankind

This discussion is a simple, brief review of the fourth book in this series, *Freedom through the Cross*. There are three basic enslavements, resulting from a man's first, personal sin. Jesus broke all of these enslavements through the cross, putting man back in his original position to walk with God if he chose to do so. Certainly his constitution changed with his first sin. But that change does not prevent him from walking with God if he chooses. This work on man's behalf declares the enormity of God's love for the whole world. All the prodigals have a way to come home, and the cross gives them the ability to travel it if they want to.

As book four in this series has explained, the cross of Jesus did far more than deal with the issue of forgiving man's sins. That is the conditional blessing of the cross. *Whenever a man returns to God through whatever means God has appointed, he can obtain the forgiveness of his sins so that he can walk in fellowship with God once again.* What a blessing to have an open door back to God and to have Him long for us to walk through it just as the father of the prodigal son waited longingly for his son's return.

In addition to this conditional blessing of the cross, there are three unconditional blessings of the cross. These solve issues that would have remained true of man if God had not graciously solved all of them for every single person. One was the *separation* from God that resulted from man's first sin. If God had not solved this dilemma, man, apparently, would have been *spiritu-*

ally separated from God throughout his entire life on earth. There is not the slightest hint in the context of Genesis two and three that this consequence of man's first sin is eternal in nature. In fact, there is no indication that the separation or death that resulted from Adam and Eve's first sin was even *temporally permanent* (i.e., a permanent condition until they were born again).

They, and their descendants after them, had no requirement laid upon them that needed to be fulfilled before they could be restored to fellowship with God. There is no indication that their sin resulted in an *eternal* separation from God. The *separation* from God that is mentioned, *this death*, is true of man only when he is actively and specifically sinning against God.

Paul made it clear in Eph. 2:1-3 that man is dead *only* in the sphere of his sins and trespasses (that is, while he is sinning or trespassing God's will). If this *dead state or condition* had not been solved by God through the cross, man would have been unreachable by any means except the sovereign, efficacious grace of God. Unfortunately, this is the only kind of grace that Reformed soteriology propounds, one that is sovereign, picking and choosing its recipients, and one which cannot be resisted when offered.

God does indeed use His grace just this way at times. For example, He used it this way when He sent one of His holy, warrior angels to slay 185,000 soldiers besieging Jerusalem. He used it again when He heals the sick or answers prayers that are not seeking to obtain His promises but are asking for additional blessings instead. But it is impossible to see this kind of grace involved when a person trusted in God in the OT for justification. Nor is this kind of grace involved when a person trusted in Jesus in the NT for the gifts of eternal life and the Holy Spirit (or for the use of those gifts in walking with God). In fact, there is every reason to believe that God does *not* use His grace in this way to bring about the exercise of faith in man.[1] He doesn't need to because the cross of Jesus made it unnecessary for Him to do so. The cross has already freed all men from the continuation of this spiritual death or separation from God.

Because of the work of the cross, this spiritual separation from God is solved for man. God is already reconciled to the whole world through the death of Christ Jesus.[2] There is no natural barrier between God and man, preventing man's return to Him. God is ready to receive all who come to Him. Every man's past is known by the omniscient God in detail, and yet He wants all to come.

By God's gracious provisions in the cross, man is fully able to respond to God whenever he is not in the process of sinning already. But even at that moment he can respond by faith to God's overtures toward him and leave behind the *spiritual death* that has been his experience while he was sinning. Spiritual death is not man's natural state or condition; it is only true of him when he is sinning.

In addition, it can be said that man's entire human nature is not sinful; only indwelling sin is sinful. The Bible never even uses the term *sin nature* to describe man's complete human nature. But it speaks very clearly about an indwelling entity which *is a part of man's nature*. And this entity is called indwelling sin. This part of man must be kept from ruling over the other *members* of his nature (mind, emotions, will, physical body, conscience).[3] These *members* can produce *good works* when they are

---

[1] I recommend a new book by Curtis Tucker called *Damn Shame* which covers this topic.
[2] 2Cor. 5:18-19.
[3] Rom. 6:12-13.

controlled by God's Spirit as a result of walking by faith in Him. They can also produce *sinful works* by being controlled by indwelling sin.[1] The cross gives man the freedom to choose which controlling entity he will believe in and obey. Both are vying for lordship or mastery over his life. As a result, relative to the sins in our lives, our consciences either accuse us or excuse us depending upon which master is ruling within.[2]

The cross enables a person to avoid the spiritual death that results from committing subsequent, personal sins by overcoming the cause of all personal sins. *The cross frees man from the necessary bondage to indwelling sin.* It does this once-for-all. Man can still live in bondage to indwelling sin, but, because of the work of the cross, he doesn't have to be enslaved to it.[3] If he simply responds in faith to God's overtures toward him, he would have constant victory over indwelling sin, keeping him from sinning and from the spiritual death (or temporary separation from God) that results from each sin a man commits.[4] *Spiritual death is not a barrier from returning to God; it is a barrier to experiencing the blessings of God presently.*

There were many righteous men in the OT who knew little to nothing about the coming Messiah. They show us what is possible for a man who lives by faith in God. A righteous life was possible before the Messiah came with His enormous, additional resources of eternal life and the gift of the indwelling Holy Spirit. God would, indeed, be partial if He required faith in a coming Messiah from those who had not been given any revela-

---

[1] Rom. 6:16.
[2] Rom. 2:14-16; 7:19-25.
[3] Rom. 6:6-7.
[4] Rom. 6:23; Js. 1:14-15.

80

tion that such a Messiah was being sent in the first place.[1]

In the NT, the Messiah came to offer the promised Kingdom[2] and to give a life that would be *a taste of that kingdom age* even before that kingdom is actually set up.[3] This life, which is experiential in nature, was one of the most powerful evidences in the first century that Jesus was the Messiah and had come to set up the promised Davidic Kingdom. When He gave a person an experience of *kingdom life* while He was offering the kingdom, those who saw the extraordinary nature of this new life in those who possessed it would be drawn to believe in Jesus as Messiah too. Hence, Jesus sent out those who possessed this life to proclaim the fact that the promised kingdom was at hand.[4]

The OT saint, even the one who believed that a Messiah was being sent by God, did not have access to the Messiah's gift of life in any way. Having Christ's life within, administered by the Holy Spirit, creates a wholly different enablement and a preview of what life in the kingdom will be like. Each moment a person walks by the Spirit of life,[5] not only is *indwelling sin,* often referred to as *the flesh,* successfully opposed, but a capacity is granted to the one trusting the Spirit that supersedes his natural capacity to respond to the situation at hand.[6] The *believer,* the one trusting at a given moment, is rightly described as not living by his own resources but living through those provided to him by Christ Himself.[7] The term *believer* does not refer to a once-for-

---

[1] Cf., Acts 10:34-35; Rom. 2:11-14; 3:29-30; 9:30-33.
[2] Matt. 3:2; 4:17. Hence, the *gospel* of Jesus was connected to *this* promised kingdom (Matt. 4:23; 9:35).
[3] Cf., John 6:47 and John 10:10 with Heb. 6:4.
[4] Matt. 9:35-10:7. Notice that Judas was among those sent out.
[5] Rom. 8:2.
[6] Rom. 8:35-37.
[7] Rom. 8:4-6; 6:23.

all belief in Jesus as Messiah, as Savior, or as Lord as is usually assumed. The term refers to one who has, is, or will soon believe Jesus for something that He is offering to him, like an answer to prayer, or wisdom needed to walk wisely, or love for loving a person that he has been unable to love up to this point. But the term never simply designates a person who has trusted in Jesus for eternal life in the sense that we typically use those terms today.

With the enslavements to spiritual death and indwelling sin overcome, man is free and capable of responding to God's overtures throughout his entire life. *The original purpose of God in creation is maintained by the accomplishments of the cross.* Man can walk with God and represent Him in all that he does. The accomplishments of the cross have been distributed by God from the time of Adam and Eve to every man living today. God never intended for man to remain separated from Him.

In some way, the precise details of which the Bible does not explain, we are led to believe that the cross also accomplishes a victory for every man over the angelic forces. There are, nonetheless, several Biblical facts that lead us to that conclusion. First, all the kingdoms of the world were Satan's to offer to Jesus in the third temptation recorded in Matthew's Gospel. What does it mean to belong to Satan? What are the ramifications of such a condition?

Second, Paul says that God triumphed over (lit. disarmed) the rulers and authorities through Christ's work on the cross.[1] They were never any threat to God. But we have lots of evidence that they are to mankind. But the book of Job explains that Satan has only the freedom that God allows him to have. While that

---

[1] Col. 2:15.

freedom can become a threat for anyone, the cross has given the one who walks by faith victory over him.

Third, the apostle John tells us that Satan was defeated through the cross,[1] and while he has already been judged,[2] the execution of that judgment awaits a future time in God's program. As a result, it seems that God wants us to conclude that due to the work of the cross mankind is not Satan's de facto possession.

In exactly what way this slavery was overturned is not disclosed to us. But that the cross overcomes Satan, the ruler of this world, and enables all men to be drawn to Jesus is clearly stated by the apostle John in John 12:30-33. God's love for all men is so powerful that He would not for a moment allow Satan to have dominion over any of His creatures as a result of their first sin. Indeed, there are consequences to every person's first sin, but an unavoidable enslavement to Satan or to any of his demonic hosts is not one of them.

God who created man for fellowship and for dependent representative service did not allow Satan the prize of man's enslavement as a result of each man's first sin. But it cost God the price of His Son's death on the cross to secure man's freedom.[3] Oh, what love is this that God has demonstrated for all of His creatures!

These freedoms have been granted to each and every man in the same way that forgiveness of sins has been granted in the OT even though there was never a sacrifice that could actually take away sins.[4] God forgave in the OT by tapping into the ac-

---

[1] John 12:31-32.
[2] John 16:11.
[3] 1John 4:10.
[4] Heb. 10:1-4.

complishments of the cross before it ever historically took place. In the same way, God freed man from spiritual death, from indwelling sin, and from Satan by tapping into the cross before Jesus ever died upon it historically.

All of these benefits, and many others, are based upon the cross of Golgotha. If Jesus had not died upon it, man's plight would have been what orthodox Christianity traditionally says it is. But the cross actually makes all those traditional, doctrinal affirmations impossible. The most relevant issue that relates to the topic at hand is this: *none of these three benefits are based upon faith in Jesus even though they are all based upon the death of Jesus.* God in His unbounded graciousness gave these blessings to all men, even to those who have never heard of the person named Jesus much less have believed in Him.

Chapter 8

Jesus, a Scapegoat? Or Not!

The most popular reason, and for some the *only* reason, that many have believed in Jesus is unfortunately *not* mentioned in the Bible straightforwardly, with the exact wording that could make its acceptance unassailable. Yet, Sunday after Sunday, one can hear this reason repeated from the pulpit of most conservative, evangelical churches in America. It is *the ubiquitous assumption* that Jesus came to die on the cross in the place of each person who believes in Him. This substitutionary death accomplishes two things, it is hoped: 1.) Jesus can forgive that person's sins (and the supposed penalties resting on those sins) and 2.) give His own perfect righteousness to that believer so that God can guarantee him a place in heaven with Him forever. This two point summary is *the gospel* in the mind of most Christians.

These widely-held, soteriological reasons for Jesus' first advent are established tenets of orthodox Christianity. To question them is to practically invite the charge of heresy upon the questioner. But these almost universally held convictions are, nonetheless, unsupported by the Scriptures. There is no passage that states those ideas together, nor are there separate passages that can be marshaled that *explicitly* set forth those elements in plain straightforward terms separately. At every turn *a mountain of assumptions and conjectures* is needed before these tenets can be found in the Bible. Here is a quick test to show the reader what is being said here.

Where, for example, would you go to find a verse that *explic-*

itly says, Jesus died *in the place of* anyone? Supposedly a couple of prepositions (αντι, υπερ) *could* say something to that effect. But the greater probability is that they don't. And it isn't like God couldn't have said it in so many words (even without using these two prepositions), right? But He doesn't.

Where would you go to find a verse that *explicitly* says there are *eternal* penalties resting upon the sins a person commits? It is now common knowledge, I think, that there is no Hebrew term or Greek term that is equivalent to the English term *eternal* and to the English concept of *eternity.*[1] Couldn't God have simply said that the *recompense* (a good Biblical term) for each and every sin continues after physical death and lasts as long as that person has an existence or life? But He doesn't.

Where would you go to find a verse that *explicitly* says a *perfect* righteousness is needed before a person can go to heaven? Do we need to revisit the debates in church history between the Protestants and the Catholics over the meaning of justification? The Protestants concluded that a person was *declared* righteous but not *made* righteous in justification. The Catholics considered a person to be *made* righteous at the moment of faith, a righteousness that could be lost entirely in apostasy. But both agreed that a *perfect righteousness* was needed for a person to gain a heavenly destination. Could it be that both sides had part of the truth, but no side had all of it? Couldn't God have said just one time that *a perfect righteousness* is needed in order for a person to be admitted into heaven? But He never does. Being righteous is not synonymous to being sinless in the Bible.

Where would you go to find a verse that *explicitly* says *by*

---

[1] R. Laird Harris, Gleason L. Archer, Jr., Bruce K. Waltke, *Theological Workbook of the Old Testament*, 2vol., Moody Press, Chicago, 1980, 2:673. Surely after forty years the research of such eminent scholars should have been well disseminated.

believing in Jesus a person obtains the gift of heaven (or a heavenly destination)? If the other points above didn't interest you, surely this one does! This one is central to all orthodox, Christian truth, right? Since obtaining a guarantee of heaven and a promise of escaping hell is really the primary motivation for many people to trust in Jesus in the first place, these verses ought to be so numerous that they just jump into one's mind readily. How easily God could have said this truth (if it is a truth at all) for us. But He doesn't. Man must connect a lot of disassociated dots and concepts to draw this conclusion. Is man's reason really that trustworthy in such a pursuit as this?[1]

Where would you go to find a verse that *explicitly* says *forgiveness* of all the sins that a person has committed or will ever commit is obtained by believing in Jesus? God has ordained a variety of means for man's employment to obtain forgiveness of his sins.[2] Believing in Jesus is never *explicitly* stated to be one of them, however.

As I have already shown in volume four, Jesus did come to die as a *propitiation* for man's sins. He did die so that man's sins could be *forgiven*. He did die to make *redemption* and *reconciliation* possible. The cross deals completely and efficaciously with so many issues.

Nevertheless, Christ's death is never said to guarantee to the man who believes in Jesus a heavenly destiny. As far as the Scriptures *explicitly* state, Jesus' death does not pay man's "eternal" debt for sin for one simple reason: *there is no eternal debt attached to his sins in the Scriptural record.* Where is such a debt ever mentioned in the Bible? What verses would you give that *explic-*

---

[1] Isa. 55:8-9; Deut. 29:29; etc.
[2] See the discussion of some of those means in my book, *Freedom through the Cross*, Firmly Planted Publications, Dallas, Texas, 2015; pp. 71-80.

itly and straightforwardly say Jesus died to pay a debt that would have lasted as long as man existed in the afterlife. Can you offer a passage that doesn't need any *assumptions* or *conjectures* for it to affirm that God requires a payment *from man* for the penalties that rest on each and every one of his sins? Can you offer a passage that *explicitly* says that if God does not receive a payment from each person, He has no alternative but to send that person to hell for as long as he has an existence?

Don't you find it interesting that those verses don't just leap into your mind? These concepts are so central to orthodox Christianity that a person has the right to expect a lot of straightforward confirmations from the Scriptures of these *supposed* facts. Is the Holy Spirit failing in His responsibility to bring to your mind what Jesus taught?[1] Maybe He can't bring them to mind if they aren't actually present in Jesus' teachings (nor in the rest of the Scriptures as well).

The fact is Jesus didn't come to take man's place upon that cross; He came to fulfill God's will upon that cross in paying the divinely required propitiation for man's sins.[2] The propitiation that Jesus made upon the cross[3] enables God to be reconciled to man[4] so that He can offer forgiveness to him throughout his life upon this earth. This proposition can be easily proven from the Scriptures. But the supposition that Jesus' death was *vicarious* is a conjecture rooted in man's reason, but not in the requirements of the Scriptures. God never intended to send Jesus to be man's *scapegoat* for a guaranteed eternity; He was, however, an efficient *scapegoat* for a lifetime of fellowship with God. Jesus

---

[1] John 14:26.
[2] 1John 4:10.
[3] 1Cor. 15:3-5.
[4] 2Cor. 5:18-21.

Christ's death deals with time, not with eternity. If we don't learn to live in the present, we won't have a very happy future.

God the Father never intended for Jesus to take man's place on the cross, dying in his stead. *God intended Jesus to die so that all mankind could die with Him on the cross!* That is a critical statement so let me repeat it. God intended Jesus to die so that all mankind could die with Him on the cross. Mankind's death on the cross with Jesus has nothing to do with the forgiveness of personal sins or with the payment for personal sins. But it does have to do with the issue of indwelling sin (along with the issues discussed in the fourth book in this series). God designed the death of His Son to be the vehicle through which all men could be freed from indwelling sin[1] because they had died to it when they died with Jesus on the cross.[2]

Physical death delivers a person from the necessary control of indwelling sin altogether. So, by uniting all men to the death of Jesus, God could free all men from the necessary reign of sin within. This is God's accounting; this is God's reckoning perspective. Initially believing in Jesus does not accomplish this freedom from sin for man. Only dying with Jesus on the cross does that. By uniting all men to Christ's death, God reckons men to have died physically before they have actually done so. Attributing a physical death to all men, God could also attribute one of the consequences of physical death to them, namely, the freedom from indwelling sin that can result in righteous living.

Our physical death is crucial to our living a spiritual life. *We died with Christ* and must now learn to reckon upon that death so that we can reckon ourselves alive in Christ Jesus.[3] The life that

---

[1] Rom. 6:7.
[2] Rom. 6:6.
[3] Rom. 6:11.

we have "*in* Christ Jesus" is a life *from* Christ Jesus. With this life we can live a life that pleases God because He is always pleased with what He sees His Son doing, just as Jesus explained:

> "And He who sent Me is with Me; He has not left Me alone, for I always do the things that are pleasing to Him." (John 8:29)

Whether you understand all of the finer points of these statements, the main point that should not be missed is this lone fact: when God planned Jesus' death from before the foundation of the world, He always intended for all men to die with Jesus when He went to the cross. *God never planned for Jesus to die **in** man's place; rather He planned for all men to die **with** Jesus!* Man's death on the cross with Jesus frees him from indwelling sin so that he can, if he chooses, obey God in all that he does.

So, the salient points are these: Jesus' death was not in any way vicarious. He did not die so that man would not have to die. Rather, God designed Jesus' death so that all men could die with Him. God planned for something to happen in physical death, and at no other time, that aids man in living for God. So, Paul says,

> ". . . **our old man was crucified with Him** in order that our body of sin might be done away with so that we should **no longer serve sin** (for the one who has died to[1] sin is declared righteous)." (Rom. 6:6-7, my translation)

At death, in this case a death by crucifixion is in view, the body of sin is *put out of work* (translated here as *done away with*). And if the body of sin is put out of work, then indwelling sin itself (that part of man's nature that is thoroughly sinful and is

---

[1] Cf., Col. 2:20 in the NASB. To die is to be separated from something. Here the separation is from indwelling sin. So the passage can be translated: "for the one who has died *to* sin, or, for the one who has been separated *from* sin . . ." This is the point of vv. 11, 12-13, and 16.

the cause of all sinful actions) will not be served. Physical death puts the body of sin out of work. And when the body of sin is inoperative, it can't function as a master or king to be served. It can't reign and be deposed at the same time. *Physical death was designed by God to break sin's necessary rulership over man.* After death no man will be serving indwelling sin ever again. (That is the reason that all men will one day bow before Jesus to acknowledge from the heart His Lordship over them.[1]) God always intended to unite the world to the death that Jesus Christ died for it.[2]

When God united all men to Christ upon the cross, it allowed God to *view* man in a certain way. He was able to *view* man *as if* he had died physically *even before* he had actually died physically. By God's plan and design, only physical death sets man free from indwelling sin. That is, only at death is indwelling sin removed from man's nature so that he will live righteously forever. In this state he will be able to give God the praise and service that He deserves, finally fulfilling the first and greatest commandment.

With God's design in place during man's earthly life, he is able to live righteously even though he still possesses his indwelling sin. It does not have to be removed from his constitution for him to live a life pleasing to God. Although it is harder to obey God with indwelling sin still residing with man's nature, it is possible whenever he walks by faith in God or uses the resources that have been given to him in Christ. By uniting every man to Christ Jesus in His death on the cross, God has made it

---

[1] Cf., Phil. 2:9-11; Rev. 5:13. If no one will be sinning in the afterlife since man will be completely freed from even the presence of indwelling sin, it is worth contemplating what the purpose of punishment is in the afterlife and for how long will it be needed.
[2] John 1:29; 3:16; 6:33, 51.

possible for every man to live without regard to the temptations that arise from within him. *In other words, man can live as though he didn't have indwelling sin at all. Consequently, man is held accountable to live as God instructs him to live.* If man reckons upon what God has done for him in freeing him from the slavery to indwelling sin and making him alive to God (instead of continuing in the spiritual death resulting from his first sin), he can live a righteous life and receive God's promised blessings in the process.

God views man as being free from the spiritual separation that occurred in his first sin; He views man as free from indwelling sin's *necessary* rulership; and He views man as free from Satan's *necessary* dominion throughout the rest of his earthly life.

All men have that capacity even after they have sinned.

Reckon upon all of these blessings. That is, take it by faith that these freedoms are true of you and stand upon them regardless of your feelings or your circumstances.

Now trust in God to make you adequate for the trial that lies before you. The life that will flow into you will be that of Jesus, enabling you *to do all things well* just as Jesus did when He walked this earth physically.[1]

---

1 Mk. 7:37.

Section Four

Jesus Came to Give Life

Chapter 9

His Life is Related to His Kingship

There probably is no fact more clearly revealed in the Scriptures than that Jesus was the promised King of the Jews. He was *born king* of the Jews. He didn't have to be chosen by the people or by the reigning king. He was born into that office. Consequently, when He began His ministry, He began to *offer the kingdom promised by God to David*, and, if the conditions for the kingdom had been met by those to whom the kingdom was being offered, He would have set it up for as long as this planet was ordained to exist. That is what the description, *eternal kingdom*, refers to, namely, a kingdom that will continue until the last days of life on this planet have come to an end.

If we begin our study in Matthew's Gospel with the Magi who came looking for the one represented by a new star in the sky, we have the clearest statement any researcher could ask for relative to the purpose of His appearing. They asked,

> "Where is He who has been *born King of the Jews*? For we saw His star in the east, and have come to worship Him." (Matt. 2:2)

This baby, who was named Jesus at His circumcision, was born to be *the king of the Jews*. This baby, the son of Mary, and of Joseph by adoption, was in line for *the throne of David*. His genealogy in Matthew's Gospel proves this beyond question.

When the religious leaders quoted the OT passage to explain to King Herod the Great where the promised Messiah-King of the Jews must be born, they referred to Micah 5:2. That passage describes *a Ruler*, who is also *a Shepherd of the people*, coming from Bethlehem of Judah. A promised ruler who would be a benevolent King had been predicted, ruling with truth and justice. He would have compassion upon the people as He ruled over them. This was a promise that stirred the heart of every subject within that prospective kingdom, everyone who was eagerly trusting God to fulfill that promise, that is.

Two years before the Magi appeared, looking for the toddler who had been born king, God had revealed to Mary that she would give birth to a son. Her son would have a two-fold lineage: He would descend from God and from King David. Luke faithfully records that revelation when he wrote,

> "… you [Mary] will conceive in your womb, and bear a son, and you shall name Him Jesus. And He will be great, and will be called *the Son of the Most High*; and the Lord God will give Him the throne of *His father David*; and *He will reign* over the house of Jacob *forever*; and *His kingdom will have no end*." (Lk. 1:31-33, emphases mine)

Whenever He begins to reign, and it ought to be crystal clear that He hasn't begun that reign and rule yet since it was over Israel that He was to exercise it as *the King of the Jews*, He will continue to *rule over the house of Jacob* until God destroys this earth and creates a new one.[1] He was born king because God had promised to set Him *on David's throne* to rule over the house of Jacob, *the Jewish nation*, forever. *Jesus cannot be ruling as king anywhere if He is not, first and foremost, ruling as king over Israel because He came to be Israel's King.* His reign is specifically related to the house of Jacob even though other passages extend His rule to the whole world.[2] To detach Jesus from His rule over Is-

---

[1] 2Pet. 3:10-13.

[2] E.g., Isa. 2:2-4; Dan. 2:44; 7:26-27; Zech. 9:10; 14:9, 16; Rev. 15:3-4. Cf., Matt. 4:8-9 also.

rael is to miss the message of the Bible profoundly. Jesus can't be ruling anywhere (e.g., within the heart of man) if He isn't ruling righteously over the nation of Israel,[1] giving them peace from all of their enemies.[2] It ought to be transparently obvious that the reference to Israel shouldn't be *spiritualized* to mean *the people of God*. But some still try to make that connection mostly their theology leads them to make it.

When Jesus rode into Jerusalem the week before His death, He fulfilled an important prophecy about Israel's promised Messiah-King. Quoting Zechariah the prophet, Matthew wrote,

> "Say to **the daughter of Zion**, 'Behold **your King** is coming to you, gentle, and mounted on a donkey, even on a colt, the foal of a beast of burden." (Matt. 21:5)

Jesus, who was born king of the Jews, entered Jerusalem in the manner that the prophet Zechariah had predicted[3] so that He would be recognized as the King that He was. During this last week of ministry, Jesus rebuked the nation for not recognizing *the day of their visitation*[4] by God's promised Messiah-King. He was the king that had been promised to come, and they should have recognized Him as such.

To obtain the kingdom that He was offering to them and over which He would rule personally and physically, all that the people needed to do was repent of their waywardness and begin living righteous lives before God. On the lips of both John the Baptist and Jesus was the exact same message reminding the people of this crucial condition of repentance that was needed for God to fulfill His promise of a Messianic Kingdom:

---

[1] Isa. 2:1-4; 11:1-5.
[2] Ezek. 34:25-31; Lk. 1:68-75.
[3] Zech. 9:9.
[4] Lk. 19:42, 44.

"Repent, for the kingdom of heaven is at hand." (Matt. 3:2; 4:17)

After they had repented, they needed to follow up that repentance with good deeds worthy of the repentance to which they had come.[1] Only righteous deeds were worthy of the repentance being called for. Only an obedience which is *of faith* produces this righteousness. *Consequently, Jesus warned His own apostles that they needed righteous deeds to enter the Kingdom even after they had received eternal life* (which has been mistakenly thought to include a salvation from hell and a guarantee of heaven). No one would enter into His kingdom without righteous deeds to unlock the door. So, He warned them that . . .

"... unless your righteousness surpasses that of the scribes and Pharisees, you shall not enter the kingdom of heaven." (Matt. 5:20)

Entering the kingdom is not a gift; it is a reward for obeying God in faith. While many have tried to make this righteousness a gift from God obtained by faith alone, such an idea is actually foreign to the Scriptures. It is imported into the Scriptures because the theological grid that has been used for centuries to interpret the Scriptures demands that this doctrine be found there.

What am I saying? Simply this: *our orthodox, Christian theology setting forth the doctrine of salvation is unbiblical; it has been read into the Scriptures.* If it was not presupposed at the beginning of the process of interpretation, it would not be found in the Scriptures nor enter into the mind of the interpreter reading them.

The Bible doesn't teach a positional, permanently-obtained *standing* before God gained by one response of faith. (Remember: this one response of faith must be man's initial faith). The Scriptures only speak about a practical righteousness. God de-

---

[1] Lk. 3:3, 8-14. Repenting and then acting upon that repentance are so closely connected in Scripture that they are *assumed* to occur together. In reality they don't (Lk. 17:3-5).

clares *a particular response* that a person gives righteous, and thus *the person* giving it as righteous, whenever He sees faith in the response being given. God's declaration of righteousness, that is, *God's justification, is an evaluation by God of what man is presently offering from his life to God* (i.e., an obedience springing from faith); *it is not a declaration of what God is offering to give to man* (i.e., *supposedly* the gift of Christ's perfect righteousness).

Righteousness, as one would naturally conclude in every decision outside of religion, is simply doing the right thing at any given moment. God only adds to that idea the concept of faith, trusting in Him in the process of doing what is right.[1] When God sees our faith in Him as we are in the process of carrying out His will, He declares that *the response we are giving is a righteous one*. This, and this alone, is the righteousness for which man is responsible. It is not beyond the reach of anyone who will walk in faith in the God who has revealed Himself and His will.

It should be plain from these statements that the kingdom of heaven and salvation are two very different matters. Salvation is *a deliverance*[2] (or rescue) from something. The kingdom on the other hand is *a place*.[3] Salvation may be without works (but typically involves works). The kingdom is entered only with works. Neither salvation nor the kingdom is ever a reference for heaven or for going to heaven after death. There are different kinds of salvations, but there is only one kingdom of heaven/God. While every salvation predicted in the Scriptures relates to the kingdom in some way, they are all preparatory for it. The salvations come first; then the kingdom is set up and entered.

---

[1] See my book, *Living through Crises*, for an explanation of what exactly we are supposed to trust God for when we are attempting to carry out His desired will for our lives.
[2] Ex. 14:13-14; Lk. 1:71-76; Matt. 14:30; Matt. 1:21.
[3] Matt. 7:21; 18:3.

The Gospel writers make it plain that neither John the Baptist's preaching nor Jesus' ministry was going to result in the repentance (including the good deeds of righteousness performed in faith) that were needed for Jesus to set up the kingdom He had come to establish. Consequently, Jesus made it plain that the kingdom would be *delayed* until such a time as that condition was met by the nation. This *delay* in the establishment of the kingdom was described in Jesus' parable of the minas:

> "And while they were listening to these things, He went on to tell a parable, because He was near Jerusalem, and **they (wrongly) supposed that the kingdom of God was going to appear immediately.**" (Lk. 19:11)

Everyone, including Jesus' own apostles, was *supposing* that the kingdom was going to appear as soon as He got to Jerusalem. In fact, this is still the most popular opinion in our day: the kingdom was begun or set up at Jesus' death or upon His resurrection or shortly thereafter. This supposition about the kingdom was probably the reason Zaccheus offered to be so generous with his wealth: he wanted to meet the condition that was needed to enter the kingdom, namely, a repentant heart (and the righteous deeds done in conformity with his repentance).[1]

After His death and resurrection, Jesus was not willing to reveal *when* the kingdom would appear.[2] Even though it was still future, it would be a prophetic certainty. It will come! So, praying for the kingdom to come is just as appropriate today as when Jesus instructed His apostles to pray for its coming in the first century.[3] When He returns,[4] He will destroy His enemies,

---

[1] Lk. 19:8-10. Cf., Lk. 3:1-18.
[2] Acts 1:6-7.
[3] Matt. 6:9-10.
[4] Rev. 19:11-21.

judge all those who made it out of the Tribulation alive, and will set up His kingdom for a thousand years,[1] which from man's short life span today could be described as an *eternal kingdom* that lasts *forever*.[2]

A correct concept of the kingdom cannot be over-estimated. It is crucial for a proper understanding of the Bible as a whole and the NT in particular. But as important as this kingdom concept is in itself, it is also extremely important in helping a person to understand *the life* that Jesus came to give those who believe in Him. Now if you are impressed with how much effort both the Father and Jesus expended in making sure that Jesus' Messiahship could be easily recognized, then Jesus' offer of *eternal life* will make so much more sense to you.

Jesus came upon the scene to first prove that He was the promised Messiah. He did this by fulfilling prophecy and by having the miraculous ministry that had been predicted for the Messiah. Now as part of the proof that He was the Promised One, He grants to all who believe in Him as the Messiah *a life* that will be like the one everyone will enjoy when he actually enters the kingdom that Jesus was offering. *Basically Jesus offered* **an experience of the kingdom** *before the kingdom was set up to prove He was the Messiah and that He had the authority to offer the promised kingdom. The only condition He set for a person to receive this life was to believe that He was the promised Messiah-King.*

What a proof this was, and still is, that He was the promised King and Messiah sent by God to Israel! The whole nation of Israel was called to repentance (with reference to their sinful life-

---

[1] Rev. 20:1-7.

[2] R. Laird Harris, Gleason L. Archer, Jr., and Bruce K. Waltke, *Theological Workbook of the Old Testament*, 2 vols., Moody Press, Chicago, 1980, 2:673, affirm this understanding. No use of the Hebrew term *'olam* or the Greek terms αιων and αιωνιος requires more.

style) toward God and to faith in Jesus[1] as God's promised Messiah. As Jesus fulfilled the role of Messiah, He would be a Savior from a wicked, oppressive world[2] on earth and a King over all the world after the wicked have been removed through His salvation. Jesus gave, and continues to give, a foretaste of THAT LIFE,[3] of THAT AGE, of THE KINGDOM[4] to each person who believed in Him then, and who does so now.

This is the reason that the life Jesus gives is called *eternal* life, or more specifically, *the life of the age* (to come). *Eternal life is kingdom life before the kingdom is established.* Eternal life, then, speaks of both *righteousness* and *authority*; it produces a righteous lifestyle while it gives authority over all those things that God originally intended man to rule. Both will be characteristic of the whole world when the kingdom actually begins.[5]

A wasted life can be redeemed by living by the life that Jesus gives. By this extraordinary life each prodigal has a chance to gain *a second inheritance.* He may have wasted his life up to this point, but if he returns to God and continues to walk by faith, using the life that Jesus grants moment by moment, he can accrue a new inheritance, one that could even be larger than the one he had wasted in his prodigal journey to the far country.[6] Our heavenly Father is gracious, forgiving, and intent on restoring each of us back into the full blessings of His fellowship.

---

[1] Cf., Acts 20:21 for example.
[2] Cf., Acts 2:40; Gal. 1:4; 1Pet. 4:1-4; etc.
[3] John 10:10.
[4] Matt. 4:23; 9:35.
[5] Cf., Rev. 19:11-21.
[6] Lk. 15:13.

Chapter 10

Eternal Life, a Taste of Kingdom Life!

What we discuss in this chapter ought to be the message people hear constantly from every Christian pulpit, in every Christian Sunday school class, from every weekly Bible study, and from the books and articles that are written about the Christian faith. This is the central focus of everything Jesus did and offered to mankind in His first advent. Everything He did pointed to and supported this issue in some way. Jesus' ministry is all about *life, a supernatural quality of life foreign to man's natural state and capacities.* Because this life summarizes His reason for coming to earth in His first Advent, it ought to be the urgently communicated message being stressed in every ministry to all of God's creatures.

Certainly and without question, Jesus came to die so that the sins of all men, living in all ages from the time of man's creation, could be forgiven. And as extraordinary as it obviously is, that benefit of His first Advent, God's forgiveness of man's sins, can be experienced without any faith being placed in Jesus at all. *The OT clearly leads us to believe that faith in Messiah (or Jesus) and forgiveness of sins are not intertwined.* The same cannot be said for the new life Jesus offered to those who believe in Him. Without trusting in Jesus for the new life that He offers, no one can obtain it initially or experience it subsequently. The experience of this new life flows to the person who actively and specifically trusts in Jesus for it *after* he has received it from Him. A person may possess new life without ever experiencing the life that he possesses.

Jesus came to bring life, a life that is qualitatively different from the life that any person was born with, a life that can be experienced in degrees, a life that brings with it virtue, wisdom, and power directly from God. You can experience this life to some small extent, or you can experience it to a greater extent. Or you can experience it in all of its fullness as a way of life. The experience you have of it depends upon how much you access it. But it is yours to enjoy every minute.

Of course, if a person doesn't know how to access it, he can have next to no experience of it even though he is in full possession of it. God will always be found to be gracious though, sometimes giving an experience of it even though there is no understanding of it. But like any other discipline, the more a person knows the better he can perform, and the better and fuller is his experience.

This new life that Jesus came to give is different in so many ways that it is difficult to know where to begin a discussion of it. So, let me repeat a general statement that I have formulated some years ago describing this life as it is set before us in the Scriptures.

> "The Scriptures describe for us in symphonic form an incredible, marvelous life that has been won for us, and freely and completely given to us in Christ Jesus. But the life that may be possessed is not automatically expressed. Jesus' life offers the believer the fullness of joy that comes from walking in the presence of God and communing with Him in intimate fashion. All anxiety, fear, and turmoil are cast out and replaced by a peace which passes all understanding, a boldness which rests upon God almighty, and a contentment which is unshaken by the enticements, as well as the trials, of this world. This life is one without weakness or flaw. It takes

104

the believer beyond his own capacities and grants him complete repose in the sovereign good pleasure and providence of God. It hungers and thirsts after righteousness, ruling over all inward lusts and conquering all outward temptations. It is obedient to the revealed will of God in all things. It is dominated by humility and maintains communion with God. It manifests patience, self-control, and love in each and every situation in life. It is fullness itself."[1]

Jesus very clearly told His disciples as well as His opponents that He had come to give life to all who believed in Him as Messiah and who followed Him in faith daily. This life is "in Christ Jesus." But we can have access to it any time we want because of the spiritual union God established between Jesus and us when we first trusted in Jesus.

So, it is very important to understand that this life is not *in us* in the same way that our natural life is. It is in us due to our union with Christ.[2] But it is still *His* life, and if we want it, we have to go to Jesus for it.

In other words, it must be accessed moment by moment (or drawn from Jesus into us moment by moment, response by response). The more it is accessed, the greater the spiritual experience for that person. But a person cannot be passive in this engagement. If he does not seek it, it will not be available to him.

That Jesus came to bring a new experience of life with Him cannot really be doubted. He clearly stated this to be the case both to His disciples as well as to His opponents when He said,

> "The thief comes only to steal, and kill, and destroy; I came that they (the sheep) might have *life*, and might have it *more abundantly*." (John 10:10, emphases and parenthesis mine)

---

[1] B. Dale Taliaferro, *Living through Crises*, Firmly Planted Publications, 2003, pp. 92-93.
[2] Cf., John 14:20 to Gal. 2:20. Faith draws it from Jesus into one's life.

The thieves to whom Jesus was referring were the religious leaders who sought to lead the sheep, the people of Israel, away from the Good Shepherd, Jesus Himself. The religious leaders were attempting to steal sheep that belonged to the Father and use them for their own benefit. They were sacrificing the spiritual needs of the sheep to gain whatever was desirable for themselves or their ministries.[1] They were destroying the lives of the sheep by trapping them in a *lifeless* religion[2] that made them comfortable apart from a daily trust in and walk with the *living* God of Israel.

In contrast, Jesus came to give life. Notice that it doesn't say that He came to sustain the life that a person already possessed. Rather, He came to give a new life to His sheep. This life would become the source for every virtue, for all the wisdom, and for the power or enablement that they would need to face every situation coming into their lives. How comforting and reassuring this would have been to them as they continued to live in pastures, watched over by thieves who wanted to mislead them, and stalked by wolves that wanted to make them their next meal.[3]

Not only will God's protection and care result from living by this new life, God also promises to reward in the coming age of Messiah the one who walks by this new life today. God's divine reward is *the second inheritance* that is available to the one who has wasted his life so far. Live now; inherit in the coming age.

Now notice that the life that Jesus came to give His sheep was a life that they could have *more abundantly*. It seems apparent that the only thing that Jesus could be comparing to the life

---

[1] Matt. 6:1-8, 16-19; 15:1-6; 23:4, 14, 15; John 5:42.
[2] Matt. 11:28-30. Cf. also Lk. 10:38-42.
[3] John 10:10, 12-13.

that He was giving to His sheep was itself. Certainly, their old, natural life was not an abundant life. But their new life would be so different from their old life that it could be experienced in varying degrees of wonder.

By speaking of a life that can be experienced *more abundantly*, Jesus prepares the reader for His parable on the Vine and the Branches in John chapter fifteen. The fruit of those branches could produce *some* fruit, *more* fruit, or *much* fruit, depending only on the amount of life (sap) that flowed into it from the Vine.[1] And the amount of sap that flowed into it was determined by how much sap the branch *drew from* the vine as it *abided in* it. This is exactly like the life that Jesus offers. It is *His* life, but it can come to you. It is *His* life but you can experience it yourself. It is His life that produces the spiritual fruit for us to enjoy.

But a major conundrum presents itself with the life that Jesus came to give His sheep. Since He came to give them a new life, and since their old life was not taken away (i.e., He gave life to living sheep, not to dead sheep), each sheep has two lives or capacities according to which it could live.

About twenty years after Jesus' death, the apostle Paul would identify these capacities as the flesh and the Spirit,[2] or as indwelling sin and grace,[3] or as sin and obedience,[4] or as sin and God.[5] Since there are two capacities present in the life of each sheep, the new life does not operate automatically within any of them. It operates only as the sheep follow Jesus, trusting Him to meet their needs situation by situation. So, Jesus said,

---

[1] John 15:2, 8.
[2] Rom. 8:4-6.
[3] Rom. 5:20—6:2.
[4] Rom. 6:16.
[5] Rom. 6:12-13.

"My sheep are hearing [listening to or receiving] My voice, and I am knowing them intimately, and *they are following Me. And [so] I am giving eternal life to them,* and [in that condition] they will by no means destroy themselves [or perish] forever, and no one will snatch them out of My hand [as they experience the life that I am giving them]." (John 10:27-28, my own translation to bring out the meaning of the verb tenses, moods, conjunctions, and context)

The giving of eternal life comes to the sheep *as* they follow Jesus. If the sheep don't follow Him, He does not *give* eternal life to them. *Eternal life is not a possession like an insurance policy against hell or a reservation for lodging in heaven; it is a life that can be experienced from the moment it is received.*

But eternal life can lie dormant within. A person is *alive* ~ instead of *dead* as James described the alternative possibility[1] ~ *when* God's instructions (usually from His written Word) are received *and* followed *as* the person *trusts* in Jesus to provide all that is needed to carry out that obedience. Consequently, a person can be dead even though he possesses eternal life. No trust; no life. Unless a person is connected to God by the cord of dependence (i.e., faith), life has no way to travel to him from God.

The word of God guides; the Spirit of God, another way of saying the life of Jesus (because the Spirit's job is to infuse Jesus' life into the person trusting Him for it[2]), empowers for living. If a person who possesses new life refuses to either learn God's word or walk by faith after he learns it, his experience of the new life that he possesses will diminish constantly until he forgets its wonder altogether. At that point, he will have to start over in the process of spiritual growth and development.[3] Such a re-start would be hindered by self-pride every step of the way.

---

[1] Js. 2:17, 20, 26. The Majority Text has νεκρα instead of αργη in verse twenty.
[2] Eph. 3:16-17.
[3] Heb. 5:11—6:1.

Certainly Jesus' sheep came into possession of eternal life the instant they believed in Jesus. Eternal life is a gift that is given by grace through faith alone.[1] But neither the reception of eternal life nor the continual possession of it is the point Jesus is discussing in chapter ten of John's Gospel. *There Jesus is addressing the responsibility of the sheep to follow Jesus in order to experience the eternal life that they already possess "in Christ Jesus."* Jesus is not discussing the initial reception of this life at all. He is discussing the experience a person can have when he follows Him and lives by the life that He gives to him moment by moment.

Jesus made it clear that apart from Him His disciples can do nothing.[2] Those who have believed in Jesus and have received the free gift of eternal life can still live *apart from Him!* Those who have received eternal life may not live by the eternal life that they have received. *A person must continue to believe Him for the life he needs moment by moment as his circumstances change requiring his needs to change with it.* An ongoing, vital faith is needed in order to experience Jesus' life. Otherwise, an obedient person is simply being moral rather than spiritual. While that is not a bad thing, it is not what pleases God. Only a life of faith does that.[3]

One of my favorite questions that I like to ask other Christians is this: *what are you trusting Jesus for right now?* As you read this book? When you drive your kids to school? When you sit in a worship service not particularly moved by what is being presented to you? When you clean your house? When you are in a disagreement with your spouse?

Walking by faith is simply the means of following David's example for us:

---

[1] John 6:47; Eph. 2:4, 8-9.
[2] John 15:5.
[3] Heb. 11:2, 6.

"I will bless the Lord *at all times*; His praise will *continually* be in my mouth." (Ps. 34:1, emphasis mine)

Without a living faith in God, how can we follow in Asaph's steps when he described the point of life this way:

"Whom have I in heaven but Thee? And besides Thee, *I desire nothing on earth*"? (Ps. 73:25, emphasis mine)

The apostle Paul says such contentment comes only when one *learns* how to respond to all the events in life through *the life* of the one who indwells us.[1] *Through Him* we find sufficiency.[2] *Through Him* we realize our own potential.[3] *Through Him* we experience the boundless love of God daily.[4]

The possession and use of this incredible life is one of the most phenomenal truths of Christianity. This life will enable you to address all the circumstances in your life with peace, confidence, power, wisdom, godliness, and grace (just to name a few of the virtues that you can experience),[5] building as you go *the portfolio of your second inheritance* from God's promised recompenses for such a life lived.

---

[1] Phil. 4:10-13.
[2] 2Cor. 3:5-6. Cf., 2Tim. 2:1-2.
[3] Rom. 8:35-37.
[4] Rom. 8:38-39.
[5] 2Cor. 12:7-9.

Chapter 11

His Life is Supernaturally Powerful

Watchmen Nee, in the middle of the twentieth century, called the supernatural life that all Christians are equipped to live *the normal Christian life* (which is also the title of his book on this subject). The reason that he termed it *normal* was that it is presented in the Bible as the normal experience for everyone who walks by faith in Jesus. Unfortunately, few seem to know how to walk by faith, or if they know how, they choose not to walk that way.

Hannah Whithall Smith, writing nearly one hundred years earlier in 1874, entitled her book on this life *The Christian's Secret of a Happy Life*. She did not mean to infer that this life is some sort of secret that only some have discovered due to their own spirituality. She meant to suggest that it appears to be a secret since so few Christians are conversant with it, and even fewer, by their own admissions, seem to live it. Mostly it is rarely taught and misunderstood when it is taught.

It is important to understand that the life that Jesus gives is a supernatural life. We must not ever think that it is merely *an aid* to help a person get *over the hump*, so to speak. It is not a boost to enable one to have spiritual victory in some area of his personal life that has entrapped him until now. The Christian life is like pregnancy: you are either pregnant or you're not. So it is with the Christian life: one is either living it or he isn't. But there is no in-between; there is Biblical concept of being in a gray area. The reason for this is simple: it flows from a life of faith. One is either walking by faith, or he is not. One is either experiencing the power in the life of Christ, or he isn't. If he is, he is living a very fulfilling spiritual life.

It is a very common misconception among Christians that they are very close to having spiritual victory in some area of their lives, but, they suppose, they need just a bit more wisdom, or a bit more virtue, or a bit more power, or a bit more of that *missing something* that would assure spiritual victory to them if it was present. If they could get this little bit of help, they feel confident that they would experience the spiritual victory that they were seeking in their attempts to be obedient to God. They don't understand that *the life Jesus gives is a replacement life; it is not a power-boost or enhancement of one's innate abilities.*

This is actually wonderful news. Jesus offers us more resources because what He is calling us to accomplish is less reachable than before we received His life. What He has now called us to is the experience of *His life* in our obedience. Before we trusted in Jesus that was not the case.

God has not called us to do the best we can; He has called those who have believed in Jesus to an obedience that they *can't* give from the limitations of their own abilities. When the apostles realized what Jesus was asking from them, they begged, "Lord, increase our faith!"

This is the new higher standard that comes with the life that He gives. Before a person hears the message about Jesus and receives the new life that He gives, he could please God by placing himself and all of his members at the Lord's disposal as he walked by faith. But now, with the new life that Jesus gives, it is only the expression of that life that God desires to see flowing through the person who possesses it, reflecting the principle that to whom much is given much is required. Living by His life by necessity creates a perspective and a confidence that is out of the reach of anyone trying to live life by his own resources.

Our human capacities don't take us as far as God desires us to go. God's will today is the experience of Jesus' life in our obedience to His will. Before we received life from Jesus, we *may not have wanted* to give the obedience God called for at times;[1] at other times the obedience called for was deemed beyond our human make-up to give.[2]

When we are instructed by God to love our enemies,[3] or to forgive those offenders who hurt us over and over,[4] or to return a blessing for an insult,[5] there is nothing within us that *wants* to give these kinds of responses in those kinds of situations. And even if we try to do it, our conscience convicts us of our constant failure to fulfill all that God really wants us to do. Usually we don't even feel *capable* of doing it because our character is opposed to such completely selfless responses.

Knowing our constitution and the need for a higher level of spiritual living, God has given us resources that take us beyond our normal responses to life's situations. When we use Jesus' life to respond in unexpected ways, we demonstrate for the whole world the incredible power of God working through us.[6]

The life that I am describing is clearly *illustrated* when Jesus came walking on the water, stopping just short of the boat that held the twelve apostles. Peter asked Jesus to let him come to Him walking on the water. Jesus agreed and merely issued the

---

[1] Gal. 5:17.
[2] Lk. 17:3-5.
[3] Matt. 5:43-48.
[4] Matt. 18:21-35.
[5] 1Pet. 3:8-9.
[6] Cf., e.g., Acts 4:1-13.

command "Come!" to Peter.

Now it goes without saying that Peter had no ability to walk on water by himself. He wasn't close to achieving this feat if only he could get a little help. Peter had no capacity to walk on water at all. But all he had to do was to simply *believe that accompanying the command "to come" (in this case) was the enablement from Jesus to fulfill His command*. As a result, he stepped out of the little boat and walked on the water. An incredible feat! A supernatural feat! But a *normal* Christian experience, spiritually speaking. The path to success in the struggles of your life is the same as Peter's was.

The enablement to walk on water was not an independent ability given to Peter once-for-all. Not only did Peter never walk on water again, he didn't even finish this walk without a near-death experience. Peter had to keep his eyes on Jesus for the enablement to continue; such a response manifested the dependency needed to experience such a life. As Peter trusted in Jesus to supply the enablement, he was capable of walking on water. But the moment he took his eyes off of Jesus and focused on any other thing or anyone else, his enablement ceased, and he began to sink. *Broken trust removed the enablement being experienced. Continued trust would have resulted in continued enablement.* This is the reason that Jesus gives His life to us *as* we follow Him.

So in Matt. 14:22-33, we learn several interrelated truths about the life that Jesus came to give us. First, the life Jesus gave is a powerful, even supernatural, life. It isn't my old life *moralized* or my old life now *spiritualized*. It is not only a distinct life, but a powerful life as well. By it, I can be what God desires me to *be* while I do whatever God requires me to *do*. All at the same time! We don't grow into these kinds of responses; they are giv-

114

en to us instantly as we experience Jesus' life within.

Second, the life that Jesus gave is not an inherent experience. No one experiences the life that Jesus gave naturally. It flows through the one who is actively trusting Jesus for it moment by moment. Consequently, some will experience more of this life than others for the simple fact that they have learned to persistently trust Him for it. When Peter stopped trusting Jesus, when he began to doubt, he began to sink.

It has been correctly concluded that either faith will cast out fear,[1] or fear will create doubt, casting out faith.[2] So a successful, spiritual life comes down to the question, "Who do you have your eyes on?" Jesus? Yourself? Others? Remember that it is God who has heard your cries, whether they were audible or not, and has come down to deliver you.[3] The One who spoke this world into existence[4] is able to sustain you in every trial.[5] The One who spoke this world into existence is able to cause you to stand at all times.[6]

I've seen God do the miraculous. His interventions have been so astounding that I could only stand in awe. I've seen Him turn babies in the womb so they could be born naturally. I've seen Him unwrap the umbilical cord from around a baby's neck so he could be delivered without harm. I've seen Him provide food and housing when there was no money for either. I've seen Him heal a man addicted to heroin overnight. I've seen Him provide strangers to pull a car from a ditch and put it back on the road and then just disappear without speaking a word. I've

---

[1] John 14:1, 27.
[2] Matt. 14:27, 31.
[3] Cf., Ex. 3:7-8.
[4] Ps. 33:6, 9.
[5] 1Cor. 10:13.
[6] Rom. 14:4.

seen Him provide finances out of nowhere to the enjoyment of those in need. I've seen Him provide an education in some of the top universities in our land when there was no way the parents could afford sending either child to the school of his choice. I've seen Him answer prayers for sleep at night when a person had gone months without a full night's sleep. I've seen Him answer prayers for friends, family members, or acquaintances to be drawn to faith in Jesus. I've experienced His hand of leading in such extraordinary ways that to question His existence, His love for me, or to provide what I need to fulfill His calling in my life would never enter my mind.

I hope this has been your experience too. It is for certain that this is *the good news* that we have to proclaim to the whole world. I wonder if your particular religious background has taught you on this matter. How are we to make the world jealous if we aren't experiencing anything more than the rest of the world is? *The good news is there is more!*

Chapter 12

His Life is Transformative

Obedience can only achieve moral conformation to the norms of a particular group or standard. But God's goal is our transformation into the image of Christ. We are to become like Jesus, but not by mere outward imitation.[1] *We become like Jesus to the extent that we allow Him to live His life through us.*[2] Only by this process is Christ formed in us[3] so that we can be conformed to Him from the inside out.[4]

To the extent that *His* life is experienced, the character of the individual experiencing it is transformed. As long as *His* life is being experienced, there is no stopping the transformation that results from His life. The change of character is as sure as the rise of dough once yeast is placed into it. The process will continue until complete transformation is attained. But the process is gradual, and it is not necessarily constant. Whenever His life stops flowing through a person, the molding, transforming work of the Spirit into the image of Christ ceases as well.[5]

We must not be deceived. No one stays in the same place relative to spiritual things. Whatever level of transformation one has experienced, that level of spiritual growth can be lost due to an empty spiritual walk. A person who becomes dull in spiritual matters may have to start over in his spiritual development be-

---

[1] 1Cor. 11:1.
[2] Gal. 2:20.
[3] Gal. 4:19.
[4] Rom. 8:28-29.
[5] 2Cor. 3:17-18.

fore growth can once again take place.[1]

Think of it this way: everyone is on a *people mover*, walking in the *opposite* direction that it is moving. If you stand still, you are taken backwards, regressing spiritually. If you walk forward *faster* than the belt is moving, you make progress toward your goal. But if you walk at the same speed as the belt runs, you will have the sense of making progress but in reality you are standing still even while you are walking. Such a condition generally produces very critical individuals, more ready to judge people than to love them. Practicing the truth matures the heart and gains spiritual discernment.[2] Gaining knowledge without the practice of it enlightens the mind without enlivening the heart. But all obedience must flow from faith because the purpose of all obedience is to be *the vessel through which* God touches the world in love for good.

It is a major step forward when we realize that *the life that Jesus offers is His very own life*. So, in the nature of the case, when we live by His life, we are like Him because His life, with all of its inherent characteristics, is flowing through us manifesting itself clearly for all to see. Wonder will be created when we live by His life just like it was created when He lived His own life.

This life is likened to a sweet aroma in the Bible.[3] It is as appealing as it is amazing. It should be obvious that when Christ's life flows through us, we will appear as He was when He ministered in His first advent. When a person is inspired by another person, he might do what that other person was known to do. In a much more profound way, when Jesus' life flows through us, we naturally reflect His characteristics. He really will produce in

---

[1] Heb. 5:11-14; 6:7-9.
[2] 1John 1:6-7; Heb. 5:14-6:1.
[3] 2Cor. 2:14, 15.

118

us, as Paul declares in Gal. 2:20, everything that He desires from us when we trust Him to do it.[1]

The transformation resulting from living by Christ's life is gradual, but the availability of Christ's resources inherent in His life is immediate. We must not confuse our capability through Christ with our transformation into the image of Christ. These are not the same thing. *Our transformation is gradual; our enablement is instantaneous.* At any moment, we can experience the life of Jesus within if we only trust Him for it.

In each experience of that life will be all the resources inherent in His life. So, for example, we will have the love we need instantly to love even our enemies. We don't need to grow in our faith to respond with this kind of love. We can do it instantly, every time Jesus' life is flowing through us.

We will have peace in the most tumultuous circumstances, and patience and forgiveness in the most offensive situations. We have all that we need to respond instantly to all the temptations and trials of life, responding just as Christ would if He were physically present in our situations. This life is not the result of spiritual growth. It is the result of spiritual rest.

Our transformation (or growth) occurs over time as we experience over and over the sufficiency of His life. Without the experiences of His life, the transformation into His image cannot occur. So, for example, I have the ability through Christ *to give thanks* in every situation I face. But I will not become *a thankful person* until giving thanks by His life becomes a normal response for me. Likewise, I have the ability *to rejoice* through Christ's life within, but I don't become a naturally *joyful person* until His life of joy is characteristic of me. When I have been *trained* by the

---

[1] Cf., Eph. 3:16-17 as well.

experience of His life, I become *transformed* into His likeness.

The transformation of which I speak is not the result of anything that a person can do to himself in order to change himself. It is a radical change that comes from God working in us as well as upon us. He transforms; we display the transformation through our responses given by the power of the Spirit of God.

Watchman Nee speaks of a *detachment* that a spiritual person may experience when he is walking by faith. The concept of detachment has been very helpful to me to understand what takes place within me. I have tried to explain his concept of detachment in terms of experiencing *déjà vu*.

We've all experienced that rather unique, but strange, situation in which we have this overwhelming sense that we've *been there before*, or we've *been involved at some time in the past in the exact situation* that we were experiencing presently. It was like we could detach ourselves from the situation because it was so familiar to us and because we had already lived it at some previous time in our life. But this description only begins to explain what is occurring within us spiritually.

When this detachment occurs, it is as though we *become an observer* to the situation that is so familiar to us. We see all the actors involved, even ourselves. We hear all of the responses being given, even our own. But we are so detached from it that we sense that *we are giving responses that are, in a sense, **not our own**.* Rather, we are simply the agents or vessels *through which* these responses are flowing. It is as though Someone is using us to give His response in that situation for Him.

Our *detachment* is from our own limitations and from any necessity to rely upon them. The response is being given, but it is coming *through* us to our delight and with our agreement from

Another. This sense of *detachment* does not happen to us all the time. In fact, it may even be said to be a rare experience, yet it *illustrates* what takes place in us each time we respond by faith in the empowering ministry of the Spirit of God. Our response is not *from* ourselves; it is *from* Christ who is living His life within us because we are trusting Him to do exactly that.

We are the vessels into which Christ pours His life so that the responses that we give are truly ours but at the same time are characterized by virtues, wisdom, and power that are not at all characteristic of us. We choose to be filled up, and we choose to have responses poured out of us that come from Jesus alone. *He is the source of life; we choose to be the conduits for that life.*

If there has not been change ~ real, substantial change ~ in our character over the years since we first believed in Jesus, then we need to realize that something is vastly amiss with "our faith." I'm not suggesting that anyone's faith is spurious (false, fake, counterfeit, or illegitimate). I'm suggesting that if there is no transformation taking place into the image of Christ, then our faith is not well informed or actively vital.

A person's initial belief in Jesus is incapable of turning him into a new creature, regardless of what is generally assumed to-day. Being a new creature is a positional concept since it is true only "in Christ Jesus." But "in ourselves" we have not changed except for the fact that the Spirit of God now dwells within us. So, the issue comes down to this: we are in the process of becom-ing *conditionally* (in our character) what we already are in Christ Jesus *positionally*.

That process involves living by faith in the promises of God as we allow the life of Jesus to instantly make us into persons who can receive those promises and obey God's word. But

121

change, the transformative kind, only comes from a person's walk with God. When there is no walk, there will be no transformation. Human maturation is not the same thing as spiritual transformation into the image of Jesus Christ. The latter is accomplished by the power of God alone. But His power is conditioned upon man's choice to trust Him for that miraculous change.

Chapter 13

His Life is Sufficient for all Trials

Sometimes it seems that the trials of this life are endless. Just as we get past one, another rises up to take its place. Others seem to have no ending; they continue on and on. While this is most unpleasant, it is, unfortunately, what the Bible indicates we ought to expect. For example, Job says,

"...man is born for trouble, as sparks fly upward." (Job 5:7)

Now if you have ever sat in front of a fireplace with real wood burning in it, you've observed how the sparks from the fire are naturally carried up the chimney by the convection of the hot air produced in the fire. You hear a crackle and a pop, and soon up goes the spark, the flaming ember. Job says that all men are born for trouble in just this way. It is natural. So, expect it.

No one wants to be the poster child for Job's further observation. He says in chapter fourteen and verse one,

"Man, who is born of woman, is short-lived and full of turmoil."

We all want to avoid such a life if we can. And in one sense, we can avoid it completely. In another sense we can't avoid it at all. God brings (and allows) the trials our way for our *good*.[1] Ultimately, that *good thing* is to draw us ever closer to Him in our walk which will gradually conform us into the image of Jesus Christ. So, when trials come, He has given us the resources to handle them in a way that keeps them from creating turmoil *in*

---

[1] Cf., Ps. 119:67, 71, 75.

our hearts as we are being transformed by God's Spirit into the likeness of Jesus.[1] The resources to handle our trials are all resident in the *life* that Jesus gave us the moment we trusted in Him.

To use Paul's concepts we can put the matter this way: the life that Jesus gives keeps us from being *crushed* when we are afflicted; it prevents our *despairing* even though we may be thoroughly perplexed over our trial; it shields us from the sense of being *forsaken* even as we continue to be persecuted; and it keeps us from being *destroyed* even when we are struck down.[2]

Wouldn't you like to live a life without fear or anxiety?[3] Wouldn't you like to experience peace even in the most stressful situations?[4] The life that Jesus has given enables you to do all this and more. If you believe that God's promises to you can sustain you through all of the threats and intimidations that can possibly arise, then this *life* will be your constant experience. With our minds we believe in the sufficiency of this life;[5] with our wills we rest in that sufficiency, experiencing an adequacy that is not our own.[6]

It comes as no surprise that this life cannot be lived without a dependent spirit. What we see *around* us[7] and what we feel *within* us[8] usually cause us to question what God says *to* us. Our emotions are as inconstant as the circumstances, that come our way, are different. And what we see never includes the presence of God,[9] and rarely the presence of His angelic resources sent to

---

[1] Cf., John 14:1; 1Cor. 10:13; 2Cor. 3:18; Rom. 8:28-29.
[2] 2Cor. 4:7-11.
[3] Matt. 14:27; Matt. 6:25-34; Phil. 4:6-7.
[4] John 14:27.
[5] Phil. 4:13.
[6] 2Cor. 3:5-6. James says *works* complete *faith*. They are different, but connected in life.
[7] Cf., 1Sam. 13:11-13; 2Cor. 5:7.
[8] Cf., Matt. 6:25-34; John 14:1, 27.
[9] John 1:18; 4:23-24; Heb. 11:6.

minister to us.[1] Some have seen these things,[2] however, and their experience was intended to be sufficient for those of us who have not seen these things personally.[3] In place of these experiences, God has given to us a far greater source of authority and certainty: His infallible Word.[4] In that mirror, we can see God as He really is every day.[5]

So, Paul described us as vessels *designed to contain the life* that Jesus gives.[6] We weren't made to originate that life or achieve that kind of life by what we do. We were made to contain an ever-constant influx of His life so that the fruit that it bears within us can be poured out upon those around us as He leads. Like any other vessel, if the living water is not poured out, it will soon evaporate, leaving us empty and incapable of fulfilling God's calling upon us to impact those around us.

How do we get filled up with this life? We get filled with Jesus' life by trusting Him to provide it to us. What He has already promised to give us will be ours each moment we trust Him for it. The youngest believer and the most mature believer have the same access to this life and can draw upon it in the same way: by a simple trust in Jesus (or the Spirit) to provide it.

Look at just some of what the life of Jesus provides in Gal. 5:22-23. It is called the fruit of the Spirit because the Spirit of God does indeed produce it in our lives. But He produces in us what Jesus has promised to us. So, He takes from Jesus what He has promised to give and infuses it into those who are trusting Him (either Jesus or the Holy Spirit) for what He had promised

---

[1] Cf., 2Kgs. 6:15-17; Heb. 1:14.
[2] Cf., Ex. 33:17–34:7;
[3] Cf., Cf., Matt. 17:1-9.
[4] 2Pet. 1:16-21; Lk. 1:1-4.
[5] 2Cor. 3:18.
[6] 2Cor. 4:7; cf., 2Cor. 3:5-6.

to give.[1] The only thing that can stop the flow of these blessings is that faith should cease being expressed in Him.

The difficulty in living this all-sufficient life is almost completely emotional. We hear from many sources both within and outside of Christendom that to handle life's difficulties, we need help that goes beyond the spiritual. In short, Jesus has not promised us, and the Spirit cannot provide to us all that we need to handle the trials that we face. All of these voices are really the agents of the evil ventriloquist who first said to Eve, "Has God said . . .?"[2] So, we become convinced that the life Jesus offers is *not* all we need by listening to the opinion of these experts who unwittingly pass on to us what Satan would have us believe.

But if we were really transparent, we would admit that we have not found those suggested solutions from all the experts to be helpful. Their promised solutions have turned out to be illusions of deliverance that evaporate in the heat of battle and then reappear to encourage us to reenter the battle and try again. All of these suggested solutions put the onus upon us to win the spiritual victory. We must realize that God never wanted us to think that the battle was our own.[3] There is only one way of deliverance in the Bible: God blesses those who trust in Him for the deliverance they are calling upon Him to provide.[4] That is what we must do.

---

[1] Cf., John 16:12-15.
[2] Gen. 3:3.
[3] Cf., Zech. 4:6; Prov. 21:31.
[4] Jer. 17:5-8.

Section Five

A New World View

Demands

A New Witness

Chapter 14

God's Original Purpose for All Men

God's plan for mankind may be compared in a limited, narrow sense to the individuals on a cruise ship. There are activities provided by the cruise line for the passengers to be involved in if they so choose. But a person does not have to be involved in any of them. He can just sit on the deck and read or sleep to his heart's content. Each person can choose whatever he would like to do, and while his choices may affect others on the cruise, none of his choices will deter the ship from reaching its port of destination because none of his choices are related to the operation of the ship or to its stability. This ship is run by a divine Captain whose plans for the ship cannot be overturned. Each passenger's choices relate to life on the ship, but not to the functioning of the ship or to the ship's ultimate destination.

Somehow, in ways that are far beyond me, man's choice and God's sovereign plan for planet earth are represented in a similar way. Man has choices that affect himself and anyone else with whom he may come into contact. Yet God is still in control over the entire voyage of the ship. God can intervene at any time and do anything that is consistent with His nature and with His will. But God's actions never remove man's personal responsibility or his full accountability for the actions he gives. *God's sovereignty cannot be unjust or unloving in any way* because these attributes are aspects of the nature of God and define not only what He is like, but also what He is able to do. Consequently, since God alone is true[1] and He alone is the Judge of the whole world, He must always do what is right or just.[2] Since He is also love (not just loving, but love itself), He can never do anything unloving.[3] So, God's sovereignty can never go beyond the dictates of His own attributes (or character traits) requiring both love and justice.

Each person's choices aboard the ship are guided by the stated conduct required by the cruise line while aboard the ship as well as by international laws. Both the ship's rules and the international laws governing the conduct on the ship represent God's desired will for man as he lives his life upon planet earth. When a person acts contrary to the rules of the ship or if he should break some international law, he is held accountable both during the cruise and after it has reached its destination.

Even when the cruise ends, if a person had broken the outlined code of conduct during the cruise, he must stand before a court of law and be tried for his actions. The judgment, that he must face at the end of his cruise, will have nothing to do with *what he believes*. His judgment will only cover *what he has done* while he was on board the ship. No one can take another's place before this Judgment Seat. Each person will give an account for himself[4] as he stands there alone to receive his just and loving verdict for how he had conducted his life.

It will not matter in the least how a person got onto the ship. He could have paid for his own ticket or received his ticket as a free gift; he could be travelling alone or in a party; he could be traveling economy or first class. But however he came to be on

---

[1] John 17:3.
[2] Gen. 18:25.
[3] 1John 4:7-8, 16.
[4] Rom. 14:10-12.

board, and in whatever state he was privileged to travel, none of these things determine what he will experience at the port of destination if he has not followed the prescribed rules of conduct. Regardless of how a person got on board, or of what he might have come to believe while he was on board, his judgment will be limited to how he conducted himself during the voyage.

What God put in place in the first two chapters of Genesis describes the purpose and the general guidelines for all of man's responsibilities while he is on his earthly voyage. God revealed His purpose, and He made sure that each person had all that he needed to fulfill that purpose for the entirety of his life. What are the specifics of God's revealed purpose? Did God change His plan for man after man sinned against Him? Can man stray from God's plan? Did God's attitude toward man change after man sinned? The answers to these questions form the message that needs to be given to the whole world.

My goal is to help the reader discern what that message ought to be without using any *conjectures* or making any *assumptions* to help the facts *make sense*. The facts already make sense. They need to stand alone without the artificial systematizing that is so difficult to avoid in our Christian sub-culture. When the facts are allowed to speak for themselves without any attempt to force them into *a preconceived mold of Christian orthodoxy,* a very different message is discovered. That message describes God's love, acceptance, forgiveness, and provision for an extraordinary life! And that is the message the world needs to hear! And that is the message that changes lives.

Until fairly recently, the last twelve years or so, I have ignored the objections from several sources to my understanding of the Bible. Verses, that would not be harmonized with the teachings that I had received, continued to prick my conscience. The cries of hurting people, who were deeply troubled about, even hurt by, the message that they so often heard. And because this message was considered orthodox and thus unquestionable, it was proclaimed with all confidence as the truth of Scripture.

My disconcertion grew the further I researched the matter. The following discussion and the next three chapters are a brief summary of what I discovered. You will be shocked, then amazed, and finally delighted over the message that God has ordained to be preached to all of His creatures. It is a message of God's love and provisions, a message of supernatural life that gives meaning and purpose to the one experiencing it, and a message of forgiveness and usefulness regardless of your past. The divine remedy is as far reaching as the problem is.

Created in His Image for Fellowship and Service

When the triune God created man in His image,[1] according to His likeness,[2] His purpose for him was three-fold: he was *to rule*; he was *to multiply*; and he was *to represent God* in all that he did.[3] A person represents God when he carries out God's will[4] in a relationship of dependence upon Him.[5] Because of how man was created and because of the purpose for which he was created, *all men seek after God during their lifetime.*[6] In fact, God judges

---

[1] Gen. 1:26-27.

[2] Gen. 1:26.

[3] Gen. 1:26, 28; 3:1-6. Man represents God by obeying Him in faith.

[4] Gen. 2:15.

[5] Heb. 11:1-2, 6.

[6] Acts 17:26. Because of how man was made (Gen. 1:26-28), and because of God's purpose for placing man on this earth (Acts 17:26-28), *all men seek God*. This is the reason God continues to communicate to him: because he can, and desires to, respond to God.

them as evil and worthy of temporal condemnation *if they don't seek Him*.[1] What kind of God would God be if He required from man what he was unable to give and then eternally condemned him for his failure? While we are to always have a fear of God, it is not supposed to spring from such abhorrent thinking.

Life is not about trying to make it to heaven or of escaping hell. Of course, everyone wants to do that, but that is not the dilemma or thematic message set forth in the Scriptures. If it were, then there ought to be plenty of verses that *explicitly* set this motif forth.

Most conservative, evangelical Christians would reject the premise set forth in several recent movies such as *The Da Vinci Code*. Yet many of those same persons are forced to treat the Scriptures as though there were hidden codes that must be discovered and properly understood because the *explicit* presentation of a heaven and hell message is not transparently present in the Bible. It must be formulated or constructed by connecting disassociated dots and by redefining various terms so that such a message can be created.

God, Partial in His Judgments?

Furthermore, if there was a designated way to attain heaven and escape hell set forth in the Bible, and if that way was limited to believing in Jesus, then mankind must hold God responsible for creating persons whom He had foreordained to live in places where He knew the gospel of Jesus would never be preached. By ordaining their habitations in areas where He knew the message

---

[1] 2Chron. 12:14; 15:12-13, 15. None with whom I am acquainted would take all of the people addressed here, limited as it may ultimately be, to be capable of fulfilling this command to seek God. So, in principle, it applies to the whole world as well as to the nation of Israel.

of Jesus would never come, He effectively created some people for hell because they would never hear the message that, if received, might deliver them from it. But the true God loves the whole world[1] and desires all men to come to a knowledge of the truth.[2] God is impartial; He does not play favorites.[3] He longs for every prodigal to return home. He is waiting on them still.

The true God is the Source of all life,[4] the Giver of all blessings,[5] and the impartial, righteous Judge of the whole world.[6] He simply cannot condemn people who had *no capacity* to respond to a message that would have secured their temporal happiness (*eternal* felicity is a motif driven by our theologies, but not of the Scriptures) as well as His own reputation.[7] Neither can He condemn people who had *no opportunity* to respond to a message that would have secured their temporal happiness and His own glory. As hard as this is to believe, God is not like the god of many of our Christian theologies when the salvation of man is being discussed. *God the Father is like Jesus*. In fact, He is exactly like Jesus who came to reach every person with His life-giving message[8] and to save him from all the wicked people refusing to repent.[9]

God created, is sustaining, and communicates with all men so that they can fulfill His purpose for them. To whom much is given, much is required. But to whom less is given, less is required. Those in other lands, living in radically different cultures

---

[1] John 1:29; 3:16.
[2] 1Tim. 2:3-4.
[3] E.g., Rom. 2:12.
[4] John 1:3. Cf., John 5:21-29.
[5] Js. 1:17. Cf., Eph. 1:3.
[6] Gen. 18:25; Rom. 2:11-12.
[7] Cf., e.g., Ex. 7:5, 17; 8:19, 22; 10:7; 14:4, 18, 25, 31; 32:9-14; Rom. 2:23-24.
[8] Matt. 24:14; 28:19-20; Lk. 24:46-47.
[9] Matt. 13:41-43; Acts 2:40; Gal. 1:3-4. Cf., Rom. 11:25-27.

with radically different world-views, are required to do two things: *to fear* (i.e., revere, honor, love) *God and to do what is right*.[1] God has revealed to them all that He holds them accountable to obey.

Most likely that revelation can be summarized and packed into just two responses: *love God and love your neighbor*. Because that is all that God required from the Jewish people to whom He had given all of His written revelation for over 1400 years, it is impossible to suppose that He would have added, or could have added, anything to that completely comprehensive, though astoundingly brilliant, summary.[2]

Why would He ever complicate the issue?

Why would God require more from those who were given so much less? If Jesus could summarize the thirty-nine books of revelation that He had given to Israel into these two commandments, it is at least reasonable that He holds the rest of the world accountable for no more than that.

The repeated motif throughout the entire Bible is that God requires from each and every person those two things: *to fear Him and to do what is right*. That is not conjecture. That is stated over and over throughout the Bible. While we may not be able to give the exact content of His revelation for doing what is right, we know that He is requiring those two things.

There is a verse in John's Gospel that summarizes the point I am making about *God's universal communication to all men*. It says,

> "There was the true Light which, **coming into the world**, enlightens every man." (John 1:9, NASB, emphasis mine)

---

[1] Eccl. 12:13-14; Acts 10:34-35.
[2] Matt. 22:34-40.

The choice to have the participial phrase, *coming into the world*, modify the *Light* instead of *every man* is unfortunate. But that understanding ultimately may not make that much difference. If Jesus can and does enlighten every man after He comes into the world, would it not be consistent to believe that He did the same thing before He became incarnate and came into the world?

If the Greek text were translated following the word order in which the words actually appear in the Greek text, the verse would read this way:

"There[1] was [already existing] the Light, the true one, [in contrast to John the Baptist's ministry described in vv. 6-8] which enlightens every man *who comes into the world*." (translation, emphasis and interpretative brackets my own)

The important point here is to notice that the participial phrase, *who/which comes into the world*, ought to naturally be seen as modifying *man* as its closest antecedent rather than *Light* which is far removed from it in the verse. The true Light enlightens every man who is born (and thus who has come) into the world. There are no exceptions.

Each man is illuminated by the pre-existent Logos who became Jesus before returning to the side of God to sit upon *His* throne (that is to say, the Father's throne). Even as the Logos was taking the form of a human being and coming into the world Himself, He was continuing to illumine all the other humans being born before Him and after Him. Astonishing! Amaz-

---

[1] The Greek verb may include the term "there" (as it could include any third person pronoun: either it, he, or she) or it may simply be translated as "was." It is, in either case, an imperfect verb denoting continuous action or presence in past time relative to the present context. John the Baptist *came* (or had come) into the world, but the Light, well, it *was already present* there when John came. Note the same use of the imperfect verb in John 1:1-4.

ing! A mystery! But such is the greatness of the incarnate Son of the Father who is the Father's anointed Messiah of Israel. Only God could accomplish such a universal task as this. And out of love only He would do so.

What the apostle John says almost in passing in John 1:9, the apostle Paul develops in Rom. 1:18-20 when he said,

> "For the wrath of God is being revealed from heaven against all ungodliness and unrighteousness of men who suppress the truth in unrighteousness, because that which is known about **God** is *evident within* them for **God** made it *evident to* them. For since the creation of the world His invisible attributes, His eternal power and divine providence[1] have been clearly seen being understood through what has been made so that they are without excuse."

While these verses are loaded with truths, there is certainly an emphasis in them on God's active communication toward *all men using the world that He has made to reveal the necessary truths to them*. What man has come to know correctly about the nature of God came directly from God Himself. Whatever was *clear* or *evident* within each man coming into the world concerning the attributes or nature of God was clear because none other than God Himself was giving that revelation.

This information about God was *clearly seen*, and clearly and *properly interpreted* by contemplating the natural creation and the orderliness of the world's functioning. God is the one giving the revelation and the one guiding each person into a correct interpretation of the information that is present throughout the physical universe. There are no mistakes or confused ideas in this communication process between God and man. Nothing and no

---

[1] Since the term Paul uses here has a suffix that denotes *agency*, I have chosen to translate the term as divine providence, denoting the hand of *God at work* in the world, rather than the usual translation of divine nature. The focus is upon the agency of God over all that He has created, rather than upon His nature *per se*.

one can thwart His purpose to communicate clearly to man.[1] This is part of what makes God . . . God! Each person at whatever stage in life he finds himself is reachable by God.

Ps. 19:1, 4 tell us that the utterances coming from the natural creation about God have gone out to *all the peoples of the earth.* Even the blind who cannot see God's creation can feel the heat of the sun[2] and know by God's illumination that He provided it for their good. In the same way that a famous artist can be recognized by the imprint of his style in his artwork, God can be recognized by His creative handiwork in nature. He guarantees this result by His direct involvement in the illumination process.

God didn't leave it to man to figure out life with all of its responsibilities, including his own innate accountability to his Creator. While he could have rightly concluded that there was a God to whom he was responsible and that he ought to obey the revelation that he was being given by that God (the cross established this capacity for all men universally), nevertheless, out of love, God not only reveals these truths to him, He convicts all men of these truths, and draws them all to Himself by teaching them what they ought to do through the natural creation all around them. As a result, God's presence, nature, and providence are recognized because He is clearly revealing these truths to all men when they think about the world in which they live.[3] Consequently, man knows innately from within himself as well as from the world around him that God exists,[4] that he is ac-

---

[1] Job 42:2; Rom. 1:19-20.
[2] Ps. 19:6; Matt. 5:43-45; Acts 14:16-17.
[3] Rom. 1:19-20; Ps. 19:1-6; 50:6-7; 97:6. Paula, a wonderful woman, wife, and mother of five, who also happened to be blind, explained to me how God used the warmth of the sun to impress her with His care and love for her.
[4] Ps. 97:6; John 1:9; Rom. 1:19-20.

countable to the God who exists,[1] and that the God who exists will reward him if he seeks Him out as he attempts to carry out His will.[2]

Nothing has changed in God's plan for man from the time the plan was originally instituted. Man was created in God's image and likeness to have fellowship with God as he walks upon this earth, representing Him in all that he does. Man was also delegated the authority to rule over all that God had created and to multiply as he exercised his delegated rulership. That was God's original intent, and it remains in place to this day. Man's job is not to find a secret, hidden road to heaven so that he can avoid hell. He job is to enjoy life . . . while he enjoys God!

---

[1] Ps. 50:6-7; Gen. 18:25.
[2] Heb. 11:6.

Chapter 15

Sin Did Not Change God's Purpose for Man

Six months after my wife and I entered the ministry right after college, I wrecked our director's car. Such a careless act might have become detrimental to our staff relationships. But that was not the case. Not only did our relationship not grow tense or fracture, it grew deeper and more profound than one would ever imagine. I learned from my director and his wife how to love unconditionally, how to place people over things, and how to forgive especially when the faux pas is not intentional. I was so moved by his loving response that it didn't take long before I considered him my best friend. Now over forty-nine years later, he remains that.

When we look closely at Genesis two and three, we ought to be amazed at the simplicity and the continuity of the relationship that Adam and Eve had with God both *before* and *after* they sinned. We find none of the things that we are told happened as a result of their sins.

We don't find God angry.

We don't find Adam and Eve condemned to hell.

In fact, we don't even read of hell being mentioned.

We don't have the death that they incurred described as *eternal* in nature (though most *assume* it is).

We don't have an evangelistic message given by which Adam and Eve could be saved if they believed it.

We don't see the need of imputed righteousness in the theological sense that is part of Christian orthodoxy.

We have no mention of Adam and Eve becoming totally depraved and, thereby, being unable to seek God or reconnect with Him as they had been before they sinned.

We don't see the evidence that an unbridgeable chasm has come between God and them.

We don't see any hoops for Adam and Eve to jump through in order to obtain forgiveness of their sins.

What we see is God seeking out the sinners, Adam and Eve, just as He does all mankind (as Jesus' interaction with the woman at the well in John chapter four confirms), and Adam and Eve, without any reparations required, responding to God as naturally as they had before they had sinned. Not only is the objective, observant reader hard pressed to find any difference at all between Adam and Eve's previous spiritual relationship with God, outside of the shame and fear that they felt when God approached them (which are emotional issues), such a difference is simply non-existent … unless, of course, it is placed into the text by the reader so that he can then find it there.

We know that *they had died*. That, God had warned them, would be the consequence of eating the forbidden fruit. But the consequence of that result (i.e., of their subsequent *death*) of their sin is difficult to find in the passage itself, unless it is the shame and fear that they now experienced. But that will hardly satisfy the systematic theologian because those consequences are simply not dire enough.

The exciting point in all this is the fact that *God didn't change His plan for mankind because of the entrance of sin into the world.* Man isn't discarded; he isn't set aside until he can be saved; he doesn't forfeit his role in God's plan for the earth. God doesn't withhold the fellowship He desires to have with man, nor does He take back the rule or dominion that He had delegated to man. Everything stays on the course that God's original intent and plan had set in motion.

Now it is interesting that David reiterated God's original purpose for man, writing thousands of years after God had initially revealed it at the time of the original creation, saying,

"When I consider Thy heavens, the work of Thy fingers,
The moon and the stars, which Thou hast ordained;
What is man, that Thou dost take thought of him?
And the son of man, that Thou dost care for him?
Yet Thou hast made him a little lower then God,
And *dost crown him [man!] with glory and majesty!*
Thou dost *make him [all men!] to rule over the works of Thy hands*;
Thou hast *put all things under his feet* . . ." (Ps. 8:3-6, emphases and brackets mine)

It seems abundantly clear that God continues to support His original purpose for man in His plan for planet earth. God *still* crowns him with glory and majesty! This seems hardly consistent with the orthodox Christian doctrine of total depravity. Whatever happened to Adam when he first sinned, and whatever may be the state of Adam's descendants, it is clear that *God values all of mankind as gloriously majestic and capable of continuing their rule over all the works of His hands in creation even in their supposedly fallen state.* According to the Scriptures then, God's purpose for man did not change in any way from the time of the original creation of the world to the time David wrote Psalm eight around 1000 B.C. The introduction of sin by man did not cause God to change His plan in the slightest.

To keep this discussion in practical terms, God's purpose for man, even after the sins of Adam and Eve, is still for man to walk with Him (possibly because he was created in God's like-ness for that reason) and to represent Him and His will in all that he does (i.e., in the exercise of his delegated dominion over all that God has created). *That is it! That is all that life is about.* God desires for man to walk so closely with Him that he is able to show the world the brilliance of His wisdom, the power of His strong hand, and the joy and peace of a life of meaning and purpose. God is forever standing at His door with His arms out-stretched, longing for all of His sons to return to Him to enjoy that kind of life with that kind of relationship.

God told Jeremiah to invite *the whole nation of Israel* to call upon Him for help, saying,

> "Call to Me, and I will answer you, and I will tell you great and mighty things, which you do not know." (Jer. 33:3)

Historically, that message would be given to only the small part of the southern kingdom of Judah that remained in the Land. There was an abundance of sin running rampant through every level of society at the time.

Is Jeremiah's message to Israel still true today? Is God's in-struction through the prophet Jeremiah to what was left of the nation of Israel *a universal principle* for other nations and peoples to claim? In this case, it seems that it is. The same principle was reiterated by Jesus during His earthly ministry. Jesus taught His apostles to pray with the same kind of assurances when He said,

> "*Ask*, and it shall be *given* to you; *seek*, and you shall *find; knock*, and it shall be *opened* to you. For *everyone* who *asks receives*, and he who *seeks finds*, and to him who *knocks* it shall be *opened*." (Matt. 7:7-8, emphases mine)

I only want to discuss two points here. One, Jesus' teaching is *universal* in its scope. He says *everyone* who asks receives. He doesn't say some or many; He says all. He doesn't even say most; He says *everyone*, a term that has both a *universal* flavor as well as a *particular* one. Every time a person asks for God's will, as long as his heart is right before God, he will receive an answer from God. Maybe this won't happen instantly; but it will occur in God's good timing. Maybe the answer will be "No" because He has greater plans than we can understand at the time.

In Jesus' teaching on prayer, *everyone* means *everyone*, regardless of his religious or cultural background. Everyone is not limited to Christians. In fact, there were no individuals who were known as Christians when Jesus gave these promises as the foundation for a successful prayer life. And what Christian does not think these promises at least *apply* to him? Each Christian is all too happy to claim these promises for himself.

Second, *Jesus says that everyone who seeks finds.*[1] That is a radical statement that, once again, hardly fits into our theology of total depravity today. We don't find any caveats given in this context. In other words, the context doesn't mention any sovereign act of God that is needed to bring a person to the point of seeking. It doesn't require the *supposed* deadness of each man's heart to be overcome first before he can begin his search. If we allow this clause to stand in all of its simplicity, it would not be able to fit into our orthodox Christian theologies today without some major, spiritual, massage work done upon it.

The text simply says *all* who *seek, find*. And since the content of the prayers is not expressly stated for the reader, we must allow the broadest range of topics possible, including a request to come to God in order to be restored back into fellowship with

---

[1] Besides Matt. 7:7-8, consider: Deut. 4:29; 1Chron. 28:9; 2Chron. 15:2, 12-13, 15; Isa. 65:1-3a; Jer. 29:13. In contrast see Hos. 5:6, 15.

Him for the purpose of once again fulfilling His purpose of ruling over the works of His hands. It is clear that God is promising a wonderful end to each man's search whatever that search may involve.

The truth may be stated in this summary fashion: since God put *all men* upon this earth to seek Him,[1] it follows that all men have the capability both to seek God *and* to find Him.[2] We must remember the point that was made earlier, namely, *God actually judges men as evil and worthy of temporal judgment **if they don't seek Him!**[3] No sin that a man might commit creates an insurmountable obstacle between himself and the God who desires his fellowship. As a result, just as God sought out Adam and Eve in the garden after they had sinned, so He continues to seek out people all over the world to worship Him in spirit and truth. God is looking for such worshippers because He knows that the cross of His Son has given the whole world the capacity to seek God, find God, and worship Him after they have found Him.

Man's personal sins do not create an impassible barrier between him and God. Whoever wishes to come to God, and all have the capability of such wishing, may come into God's presence to experience fellowship with God and find the meaning and purpose that has been so elusive up to this point.

If you haven't already, will you come? Now is the time. Don't put it off.

---

[1] Acts 17:26-27.
[2] Cf., Deut. 4:25-29; 1Chron. 28:9; 2Chron. 14:2, 4; 15:2; 19:2-3; Ps. 34:10; etc.
[3] E.g., 2Chron. 12:14; 15:12-13, 15.

Chapter 16

Man May Stray from God

After a person reconnects with God, he may not necessarily continue to cling to Him. After he returns to God, he can choose to turn from his quest of seeking God or from his relationship with Him because of any number of spiritual hindrances that can arise in his life. When he turns away from God's revelation of Himself, he may begin to create a god after his own liking.[1] As Voltaire once famously wrote satirically,

"If God has made us in his image, we have returned him the favor."[2]

All spiritual hindrances, that arise, are overcome each time a person turns to God in faith. The capacity to turn to God was provided once-for-all-time by God's gracious accomplishments through the cross for all men universally.[3]

What was the reason that God provided this capacity for all men universally? It is God's desire for all to come to Him.[4] God's work of *convicting all* men of their sin, of *providing forgiveness* for *all* men's sin through the Lamb He sent to die for the whole world, and of *drawing all* men to Himself flow naturally from the fact that He has freed up all men to come to Him and from the fact that He is continually inviting *all* men to come. In short then, because God made it possible for all men to come, He con-

---

[1] Rom. 1:18-25.
[2] Retrieved on 6/7/16 at https://wikiquote.org/wiki/Voltaire#Quotes_about_Voltaire.
[3] Rom. 6:6-10; 8:3; 2Cor. 5:18-21; 1Pet. 2:24-25.
[4] 1Tim. 2:4.

tinues to communicate with al men through a variety of means so that they have the knowledge of how to come.

God may use a vast array of means and agents to accomplish His illuminating task. So, the apostle John can write in his Gospel when he is recording Jesus' message about the coming of the Holy Spirit, who is one of His illuminating agents,

> "And He, when He comes, will convict *the world* concerning sin, and righteousness, and judgment." (John 16:8)

While the Holy Spirit was already carrying out this ministry of convicting the whole world before Jesus died, rose, ascended, now that He has been sent to be the great Helper in Jesus' place, He carries out that ministry of convicting men whenever Jesus is preached to the world. God's intention in both the ministry of Jesus and in that of the Holy Spirit is to bring men and women into fellowship with Himself. That purpose must become our focus as we speak to a hurting world because it is the central theme around which everything else revolves. Such a message will require follow up from an initial contact in order to make it a practical reality in the life of the one being it for the first time.

Even though it is the desire of God's heart for all to return to Him and walk with Him all their lives, each man can stray from God or cease his pursuit of God once he has drawn near to Him. The truth that God is revealing about Himself to all men can be suppressed so that it does not have the affects God desires.[1] As man turns away from God's revelation of Himself and His will, he by necessity becomes the authority for understanding himself and the world around him. As he depends upon himself to interpret man's nature and needs and to give meaning to life,[2] he

---

[1] Rom. 1:18.
[2] Rom. 1:21-23, 28.

finds he is incapable of doing so for the simple reason that man's psyche is beyond the reach of any tool that man possesses.[1] And as far as the universe goes? How can a finite man ever be considered capable of comprehending the practical infinitude of the earth[2] much less that of the entire universe?

The Israelites that God redeemed out of Egypt were all identified as God's own son. Nevertheless, all those over twenty years of age died off in the desert because of their unbelief. Yet they prepared their children to walk with God during the forty years that they walked in circles in the wilderness so that the children could inherit the Promised Land that God wanted them to possess.

So, when Joshua took that second generation into the land to conquer it, they are described in these words,

> "And Israel served the Lord all the days of Joshua and all the days of the elders who survived Joshua, and had known all the deeds of the Lord which He had done for Israel." (Josh. 24:31)

That would be around 1400 B.C. since the fall of Jericho, the first city that Joshua conquered, is dated then. Yet at no time were the people without sin while they served the Lord their God! *Believing in God and following Him faithfully do not preclude the presence of sin in a person's life.*

After three hundred and fifty years, God explained to Samuel that in asking for a king to be like the nations around them, the Israelites were revealing their own spiritual state. God said,

> "And the Lord said to Samuel, 'Listen to the voice of the people in regard to all that they say to you, for they have not rejected you, but they have rejected Me from being king over them. *Like all the deeds which they have done since the day that I brought them up*

---

[1] Cf., Jer. 17:9; 23:33-40; 1Cor. 2:11.
[2] Cf., Job chapters 38-41.

from Egypt even to this day ~ in that they have forsaken Me and served other gods ~ so they are doing to you also." (1Sam. 8:7-8)

All the time that Israel had served God from the time that He brought them out of Egypt, they had also served other gods as well. All the time that they had held onto the living God, they were also worshipping other gods alongside of the true and living God.

Now in Samuel's day they wanted to go further into their unbelieving lifestyle. While God knew the natural consequences of such a decision would involve much pain and suffering, He allowed them to choose their own path. He does the same today.

Another three hundred and fifty years later, God describes the spiritual state of His beloved sons this way:

"...Sons I have reared and brought up, but they have *revolted against Me*. . . . Alas, *sinful nation*, People weighed down with iniquity, Offspring of evildoers, Sons who *act corruptly*! They have *abandoned* the Lord, They have *despised* the Holy One of Israel, *They have turned away from Him*." (Isa. 1:2, 4, emphases mine)

They have been unresponsive to God's loving chastisement. God wonders in this passage where and how He can further discipline them to bring them to their senses. He sees their continued rebellion; He knows that their whole head is sick and that their whole heart has grown spiritually faint. (Yet remember that according to the Shema, it is with that same mind and with that same heart they were to love God.) So, He describes the nation this way:

"From the sole of the foot even to the head there is nothing sound in it . . ." (Isa. 1:5, 6)

If the history of Israel can be used as an evaluation as well as a template for the world, and surely that is the reason a record

150

of their history has been preserved for us,[1] then at no time has an entire people or nation lived wholly devoted lives before the Lord.

The book of Jeremiah, written about one hundred and fifty years later, chronicles the rebellion, the lack of perseverance, and the apostasy of Judah, the southern kingdom of the nation of Israel. Every chapter reeks with the gross spiritual and moral pollution of the people as their sins are catalogued. Nonetheless, it is this people to whom God promised to send a delivering, conquering Messiah who will wisely lead the nation with justice and righteousness.[2] To this same people, God promised to give a new covenant which will be instilled upon the heart, transforming the life of each person.[3]

Such has been the tendency and plight of all the peoples of the earth since the time of creation. But God's response to man's propensity to turn away from Him has been very different from the response that we would have given ourselves. Our response most likely would have been very judgmental, very critical, very retributive. But God stands ready to forgive. He longs to bless each and every person who will return to Him. Jesus portrayed God the Father as the father of the prodigal son, standing in the doorway of his house, looking longingly out into the distance, hoping to get a glimpse of his son returning home.

Why is this the proper picture of God? Why is this the kind of God that God wants us to believe exists?

Because life apart from God is *death* (Lk. 15:24, 32);

Because life apart from God is *futile* (Rom. 1:21-23);

Because life apart from God is *joyless* (Ps. 16:11; Neh. 8:10);

---

[1] Cf., Rom. 15:4; 1Cor. 10:6, 11.
[2] Jer. 23:1-8.
[3] Jer. 31:27-34.

Because life apart from God is *fearful* (Isa. 41:10; John 14:1);

Because life apart from God is *morally chaotic* (Judg. 21:25; Isa. 40:15-31, esp. v. 17; Jer. 23:36; Prov. 14:12);

Because only life with God is life indeed!

As Augustine of Hippo said in his *Confessions*,[1]

> "...thou hast made us for thyself [O Lord] and restless is our heart until it comes to rest in thee."

That comment is as close to Jesus' own words as one is likely to find. Jesus said,

> "Come to Me all who are weary and heavy laden, and I will give you rest. Take My yoke upon you and learn from Me . . ., and you shall find rest for your souls." (Matt. 11:28-29)

That was said almost two thousand years ago. There are no truer words spoken today. Thomas Aquinas, it is rumored, once said,

> "I sought the dove of peace and it flew away. I looked at Jesus, and it flew into my heart."

If you look in the right place, you will find the peace and rest that you seek so desperately. God is inviting all men to return to Him and to experience an extraordinarily different life by walking in dependence upon Him to provide a full and meaningful life. Even the greatest spiritual men throughout the history of the world have only scratched the surface of what God is offering, a life so profound that nothing can separate you from the experience of God's love for you.[2] Come back and experience the Father's embrace.

---

[1] St. Augustine, *Confessions*, Book I, chapter 1, p. 13, edited and translated by Albert C. Outler, Grand Rapids, MI: Christian Classics Ethereal Library.
[2] Rom. 8:38-39.

Chapter 17

God's Message for an Ever-Shrinking World

We have concluded that all men seek God during their life.[1] They do this because God created them for this purpose[2] and because God is continuing to speak to all men[3] so that they can still fulfill His original plan for them.[4] *That simple divine plan is for all men to walk with God as they represent Him in all that they do.*[5] God's continuing communication to man gives him exactly what he needs: directions on how to walk with God and how to properly carry out the dominion that God has delegated to him.

Since the Bible *never explicitly affirms* the idea that life is about man trying to find the *right* path to God so that he can make it to heaven, it is best to focus upon what it actually does say. God wants all men to know that He loves them and that He has provided everything they need for a successful spiritual life today. Properly living life today will gain an abundantly supplied entrance into the coming age of Messiah's earthly kingdom which is still future. That celebratory entrance into the Messiah's earthly kingdom will spill over into a sensational experience with God and service for God throughout our after-death existence with God. So, *life is all about responding properly to God now.*

---

[1] Cf., Deut. 4:25-31, esp. v. 29; 1Chron. 16:10-11; 1Chron. 22:19; 1Chron. 28:9; 2Chron. 7:13-14; 2Chron. 12:14; 2Chron. 14:2, 4; 2Chron. 15:2; 2Chron. 15:12-13, 15; 2Chron. 30:18-20; Ps. 27:8; Isa. 55:6-7; Jer. 29:13; Acts 17:26-27.

[2] Acts 17:22-26; 1Cor. 1:9; 1John 1:3, 6-7; Js. 4:7-10; 1Pet. 5:6-7; etc.

[3] Ps. 19:1-6; 50:6-7; 97:6; John 1:9; Rom. 1:19-20.

[4] Ps. 8:3-6; Acts 17:22-31.

[5] Gen. 1:26, 28; 3:1-6; Ps. 8:3-6; Micah 6:8; etc.

If we respond properly to God now, then the future will take care of itself. If we don't, the future will have unwanted and unpleasant experiences. As Todd, a man in my Thursday morning Bible Study has said in summary after re-reading the whole Bible a couple of times, "Do good; get good. Do bad; get bad." He is correct. His summary represents the basic teaching throughout the entire Bible. Faith in Jesus does not supersede that basic expectation. Faith accompanies that expectation.

So, our earthly lives are about experiencing the love God has for us. We can experience that love consistently if we walk in dependence upon Him as the OT saints did. An even greater experience of God's love can be ours if we walk by the all-sufficient resources given to each one who believes in Christ Jesus. This is an experience we do not find in the OT. As we live by faith, whether that faith is in God Himself or in the supply of supernatural resources through Christ, God blesses, in some way, in everything we do. *The earthly age to come, known as the Davidic Kingdom of Messiah, is a reward for those who have walked uprightly.* If we live a life that pleases God now, we win now and we win later in the age to come. If we don't, we won't. It is either win, win or lose, lose. Believing in Jesus at one given point for a forgiveness that covers everything you will ever do won't turn a loss (a faithless lifestyle) into a win (blessings now or in the age to come) as we have been taught all too often.

In light of those facts, what message do you suppose best fits God's purpose for man upon this earth? What message ought we to be giving to the rest of the world when we share *a Biblical faith* with them? God is looking for all men to live righteously before Him, and faithfully so. He is, or He has given, the resources to live that kind of life. To think that this mandate is

nothing to be taken seriously because of having believed in Jesus is to arrive at the Judgment Seat of God unprepared.

God has provided for all men, wherever they live and to whatever culture, religion, or tradition that they may cling, the freedom to respond to all of His overtures to them. They can believe the revelation that He gives them, and they can obtain forgiveness any time they return to Him. All these things were made possible by the cross of Jesus for all men universally.[1]

In neither Testament do we find a warning given by God to man that if he doesn't believe a certain message, he will certainly be sent to hell forever. Going to a place of torment, punishment, or chastisement was never based upon what anyone refused to believe or upon what they didn't have the opportunity to believe. *Receiving discipline in the afterlife is always related to how one lived his earthly life.* The *righteous* and the *wicked* will be given very different experiences in the afterlife.[2] Only one will be resurrected to participate in the Kingdom of Heaven even though he might have believed in God or in Jesus during his life time.

The *righteous* should be defined as those who lived by faith in God while attempting to accomplish His revealed will to them. Being righteous is not a gift; it is not a standing or permanent status before God. It is doing the right thing, the God appointed thing, as one trusts in God in its performance. From the time of Jesus onward this obedience is enabled by the life He gives to achieve that purpose.

The *wicked* should be defined as those who chose to live by faith in some other source (in themselves, in other men, in sci-

---

[1] All of these things have been adequately set before the reader in the previous four volumes of this series, being based upon the *explicit* statements of Scripture. In this summary, these conclusions are simply stated rather than defended.

[2] Dan. 12:1-2; Matt. 11:20-24; John 5:24-29. Cf., Ps. 1:1-6.

ence, in education, etc.) while seeking to accomplish what they had supposed to be good.[1] And those who are attempting to accomplish what God desires apart from faith in God will also be judged by God. The negative judgment that they will receive at God's Judgment Seat will probably come as a great shock to them. But God has given plenty of warning about following His revealed will *in faith*.[2] All who attempted to carry out God's will in the OT *without faith* were sternly dealt with by God.[3]

The message of the Bible then is a very positive one. It encourages all men to pursue God and to expect His blessings when they do.[4] The cross unconditionally provided everything each person needs to carry out his pursuit of God, including a basis for God's forgiveness of each man who has failed along the way. In addition to those enormous blessings, God is offering *new life* to each person who believes in Jesus. With this new life, no obstacle can arise that can't be dealt with in a way that is pleasing to God.

Here then is a suggestion of *a good news tract* that faithfully tells the story of the Bible and can be shared with the whole world. *First, a person needs to know that God loves him.* That love is being expressed toward the whole world,[5] and it can be experienced by every single person wherever he may live.

The lack of experiencing that love is not a sign that God's love is not real. It is, rather, a sign that there is *something* block-

---

[1] Cf., Prov. 14:12; Jer. 17:5-8.

[2] Heb. 11:1-2, 6. Cf., Rom. 14:23.

[3] Cf., Moses' attempt to deliver his people by striking down the Egyptian taskmaster (Ex.2:11-15); Nadab and Abihu offered incense but did not follow God's instructions in how it should be done (Lev. 10:1-2; Ex. 30:1-10); the Israelites give a belated obedience which God does not accept (Num. 14:1-45); Moses striking the rock twice instead of speaking to it as he was commanded to do (Num. 20:8-13).

[4] Heb. 11:6.

[5] John 3:16.

ing a person's experience of God's love toward him. That *something* is, of course, man's personal sins.[1] God even demonstrated His love for every single person in a very historically verifiable way: while all men were still separated from God because of their personal sins, He provided for their forgiveness through the death of His Son on the cross. Now all they have to do is return to Him to be forgiven and to begin experiencing God's love for them.[2]

Second, man has a natural propensity to turn away from God. While this propensity constantly prompts from within, it does not need to be followed. It can be resisted. Consequently, God holds all men responsible to overcome it.[3] Nevertheless, living by this evil propensity, called indwelling sin in the Bible, is the reason that God's love is unrecognized and unfelt. As James explains to us, if God and His love feel so far away, it is not that God has moved away, but man has removed himself from God's presence.[4]

Third, God is offering a new life that produces a new spiritual power to conquer all the spiritual trials that come into each person's life. In addition to the capability of living by faith in God provided by Jesus' work on the cross for all men, God is offering a new life to the man who walks by faith in Jesus (or the Holy Spirit). This life is not like anything man has experienced on his own. No one in the OT even had the privilege of experiencing it. This life is not only powerful so that all trials can be spiritually overcome, but it also brings joy and peace, meaning and purpose, and complete spiritual satisfaction to the one living by it.

---

[1] Isa. 59:1-2; John 9:31; Ps. 66:18.
[2] Rom. 5:8; Lk. 24:47; Acts 26:16-18.
[3] Cf., Gen. 4:7; Rom. 6:12-13.
[4] Js. 4:8. Cf., Gen. 4:16; Jonah 1:1-3.

Fourth, a person must continue to walk by faith if he wants to have a constant experience of this life and all the blessings it offers. A cessation of belief terminates the experience of this extraordinary life. Continual belief in Jesus to provide specifically what is needed in a given situation, or in situation after situation, results in the continual experience of that He has promised to give.

In a recent trip to the far East, I led two persons to faith in Jesus without ever mentioning heaven or hell. How could I do that? It was easy. Those two individuals, a mother and her son, needed God's hand on their lives *now*. They had troubles and trials *now*. They weren't concerned in the slightest, as far as I could discern, about their eternal destiny. Their concerns reflected perfectly the concerns of the people set before us in both Testaments of the Bible. While both Testaments give plenty of evidence that there is an afterlife and that all men will be judged before they partake of it, almost the entire focus is upon a walk with God now in the present age, gaining by that walk a place of service in the glorious age to come upon this earth.

What if the question of one's eternal destiny does come up? How should that be addressed? Exactly as the Bible addresses it: walk in God's love now, and continue to experience His love at the Judgment Seat;[1] follow God now in faith, and expect to hear, "Well done, good and faithful servant" at the Judgment Seat.[2] If God justifies your walk today, He can't overturn His own declarations at the Judgment Seat later.[3] Likewise, if He doesn't approve of your walk today, be sure that He will not be giving an approval at the Judgment Seat.[4] So, the answer to this debilitat-

---

[1] 1John 4:16-18.

[2] Matt. 25:21, 23; Lk. 19:17.

[3] Matt. 12:33-37; Lk. 10:29-37; 18:9-14; Acts 13:38-39: Rom. 2:13; Rom. 6:7. Gal. 2:16.

[4] Ps. 1:1-6; Dan. 12:1-2; 1John 2:28; Matt. 25:24-30; Lk. 19:20-26; 1Cor. 3:12-15; 2Cor. 5:9-15.

ing even paralyzing question of where will I go when I die is quite simple: prepare now for your judgment by walking worthily of your calling.[1]

But if anyone thinks that he has a pass at the Judgment Seat of God because of his faith in Jesus, he needs to reassess that belief. I know that such an idea has been taught within Christendom for five hundred years, but it simply does not have the Biblical support that we thought it had. You are worried about your eternal destiny only because you've been taught to worry about it. But no such worry appears in anyone in the Bible.

The question is not one of balancing the scales of your works, hoping that the good works outweigh the bad works, because you will be judged for all of your works whether they are good or bad. So, if the good ones outweigh the bad, you still have to be held responsible for the bad. If your bad works outweigh your good works, then, most likely, you already know what verdict you can expect at the Judgment Seat.

But don't overlook the forgiveness, the fellowship, and the blessings that you can still have in this life along with a promise of additional rewards in the afterlife by simply pursuing God now. While no one can undo what has been done, it is also true that no one but God is capable of judging what each person has done. Every one of us is different in lots of ways. We have different backgrounds and different amounts of divine revelation given to us. Only God can properly evaluate all the variables that are involved in a person's life. And we can all be sure that when He judges, it will be a righteous judgment.[2] No one will be treated unfairly.

---

[1] Cf., Lk. 3:7-14, 18; Eph. 4:1-3; 5:1-2.
[2] Gen. 18:25.

The good news is so very good. On top of being absolutely fair and just in His evaluations of each of us, His judgment will be covered with mercy![1] How does that work? I don't know. But it is so like our gracious, compassionate God to respond with such love. It is not a matter of how many times you may have fallen. The material issue is the way you have responded after clearly understanding what God expects. Or to put that a little differently, it isn't a matter of how you start the race, but how you finish it. Finish well and be humbled by God's response to that.

He is your loving Father who is inviting you back home today in order to celebrate life together, rather than dwell upon opportunities gone by. We all stand together as prodigals. The good news is that it is never too late to return to our Father's loving embraces.[2]

---

[1] Js. 2:13.

[2] I have put these Biblical facts into a tract that can be shared with anyone with whom you strike up a conversation. They also can be obtained through our website, E-L-M.org (standing for Equipped for Life Ministries) or our post office box Equipped for Life Ministries, P.O. Box 12013, Dallas, Texas, 75225. This tract removes the barriers that the accepted evangelistic message of our orthodox, Christian tradition has created between the Christian faith and all other peoples and their faiths. Without diluting our faith, it invites all others to join with us in a walk that enables us *to properly fear God and to do what is right*. On these two points King Solomon said all men ought to be in agreement (Eccl. 12:13-14. Cf., Acts 10:34-35).